STEINER, George. In Bluebeard's castle; some notes towards the redefinition of culture. Yale, 1971. 141p (T. S. Eliot memorial lectures) 70-158141. 5.95. ISBN 0-300-01501-1

Brief analysis of Western culture, fashionably Freudian with updating dashes of Marcuse and McLuhan, brimming with allusions, absorbed in cultural fracture and decay, in a sense concluding, on p. 34, with acceptance of T. S. Eliot's description of genuine civilization as religious yet continuing for another 107 p. of analytic overture. Steiner sees 19th-century "ennui" as having produced 20th-century wars. After Napoleon, the last hero, inspiration paled away into middle-class ineffectiveness. Western man could not abide three great Judaic challenges — monotheism, early Christian morality (which was Judaic), and messianic socialism (Marx, Trotsky, Bloch). Collective guilt led to Hitler's death camps and the Jewish "solution." Steiner is provocative and evocative; he knows all the comments reviewers will make about him. He just wants to tell how bad everything is, and why. As cultural theory, it is a bit monstrous; but so were the death camps. Steiner may get to be another of those Judaic challenges, if his thesis were to bear development. Here his metaphor runs away with him

— that last door of Bluebeard's, you know: artistic as a conclusion, but not prescriptive. Recommended as ground for arguments, lots of them. No index.

CHOICE   *MAR. '72*

Humanities

CB
428
S82

THE T. S. ELIOT MEMORIAL LECTURES FOR 1970

George Steiner is Extraordinary Fellow at
Churchill College, Cambridge, and the
author of *Tolstoy or Dostoevsky*, *The
Death of Tragedy*, and *Language and
Silence*.

We seem to stand, in regard to a theory of culture, where Bartók's Judith stands, when she asks to open the last door on the night.

YALE UNIVERSITY PRESS: NEW HAVEN: 1971

In
Bluebeard's
Castle SOME NOTES

TOWARDS THE REDEFINITION OF CULTURE

George
Steiner

Designed by Sally Sullivan and set in
Linotype Garamond type.
Printed in the United States of America by
The Carl Purington Rollins Printing Office of the
Yale University Press.

Distributed in Mexico by Centro Interamericano de
Libros Académicos, Mexico City; in Central and
South America by Kaiman & Polon, Inc., New York
City; in India by UBS Publishers' Distributors Pvt.,
Ltd., Delhi; in Japan by John Weatherhill, Inc., Tokyo.

For Daniel and Joanna Rose

A chaque effondrement des preuves le poète
répond par une salve d'avenir. René Char

ACKNOWLEDGMENT

I wish to express my thanks to the University of Kent at Canterbury and to the Trustees of the T. S. Eliot Memorial Lecture Foundation at whose invitation the contents of this book were given in lecture form during March 1971.

Thanks are due also to Mrs. Carol Weisbrod, of the Yale Law School, who saw much of the material in draft and made valuable corrections and suggestions.

G.S.

CONTENTS

1 · The Great Ennui

S ome Notes towards the Redefinition of Culture: my subtitle is, of course, intended in memoration of Eliot's *Notes* of 1948. Not an attractive book. One that is gray with the shock of recent barbarism, but a barbarism whose actual sources and forms the argument leaves fastidiously vague. Yet the *Notes towards the Definition of Culture* remain of interest. They are, so obviously, the product of a mind of exceptional acuteness. Throughout my essay, I will be returning to issues posed in Eliot's plea for order.

It is not the literal past that rules us, save, possibly, in a biological sense. It is images of the past. These are often as highly structured and selective as myths. Images and symbolic constructs of the past are imprinted, almost in the manner of genetic information, on our sensibility. Each new historical era mirrors itself in the picture and active mythology of its past or of a past borrowed from other cultures. It tests its sense of identity, of regress or new achievement, against that past. The echoes by which a society seeks to determine the reach, the logic and authority of its own voice, come from the rear. Evidently, the mechanisms at work are complex and rooted in diffuse but vital needs of continuity. A society requires antecedents. Where these are not naturally at hand, where a community is new or reassembled after a long interval of dispersal or subjection, a necessary past tense to the grammar of being is created by intellectual and emotional fiat. The "history" of the Amer-

3

ican Negro and of modern Israel are cases in point. But the ultimate motive may be metaphysical. Most history seems to carry on its back vestiges of paradise. At some point in more or less remote times things were better, almost golden. A deep concordance lay between man and the natural setting. The myth of the Fall runs stronger than any particular religion. There is hardly a civilization, perhaps hardly an individual consciousness, that does not carry inwardly an answer to intimations of a sense of distant catastrophe. Somewhere a wrong turn was taken in that "dark and sacred wood," after which man has had to labor, socially, psychologically, against the natural grain of being.

In current Western culture or "post-culture," that squandered utopia is intensely important. But it has taken on a near and secular form. Our present feeling of disarray, of a regress into violence, into moral obtuseness; our ready impression of a central failure of values in the arts, in the comeliness of personal and social modes; our fears of a new "dark age" in which civilization itself, as we have known it, may disappear or be confined to small islands of archaic conservation—these fears, so graphic and widely advertised as to be a dominant cliché of the contemporary mood —derive their force, their seeming self-evidence, from comparison. Behind today's posture of doubt and self-castigation stands the presence, so pervasive as to pass largely unexamined, of a particular past, of a specific "golden time." Our experience of the present, the judgments, so often negative, that we make of our place in history, play con-

tinually against what I want to call the "myth of the nineteenth century" or the "imagined garden of liberal culture."

Our sensibility locates that garden in England and western Europe between ca. the 1820s and 1915. The initial
date has a conventional indistinction, but the end of the
long summer is apocalyptically exact. The main features
of the landscape are unmistakable. A high and gaining literacy. The rule of law. A doubtless imperfect yet actively
spreading use of representative forms of government. Privacy at home and an ever-increasing measure of safety in
the streets. An unforced recognition of the focal economic
and civilizing role of the arts, the sciences, and technology.
The achievement, occasionally marred but steadily pursued,
of peaceful coexistence between nation states (as, in fact
obtained, with sporadic exceptions, from Waterloo to the
Somme). A dynamic, humanely regulated interplay between social mobility and stable lines of force and custom
in the community. A norm of dominance, albeit tempered
by conventional insurgence between generations, between
fathers and sons. Sexual enlightment, yet a strong, subtle
pivot of agreed restraint. I could go on. The list can be
easily extended and detailed. My point is that it makes for
a rich and controlling image, for a symbolic structure that
presses, with the insistence of active mythology, on our
current condition of feeling.

Depending on our interests, we carry with us different
bits and pieces of this complex whole. The parent "knows"
of a bygone age in which manners were strict and children

domesticated. The sociologist "knows" of an urban culture largely immune to anarchic challenge and sudden gusts of violence. The religious man and the moralist "know" of a lost epoch of agreed values. Each of us can summon up appropriate vignettes: of the well-ordered household, with its privacies and domestics; of the Sunday parks, leisured and safe; of Latin in the schoolroom and apostolic finesse in the college quad; of real bookstores and literate parliamentary debate. Bookmen "know," in a special, symbolically structured sense of the word, of a time in which serious literary and scholarly production, marketed at low cost, found a wide or critically responsive echo. There are still a good many alive today for whom that famous cloudless summer of 1914 extends backward, a long way, into a world more civil, more confident, more humanely articulate than any we have known since. It is against their remembrance of that great summer, and our own symbolic knowledge of it, that we test the present cold.

If we pause to examine the sources of that knowledge, we shall see that they are often purely literary or pictorial, that our inner nineteenth century is the creation of Dickens or Renoir. If we listen to the historian, particularly on the radical wing, we learn quickly that the "imagined garden" is, in crucial respects, a mere fiction. We are given to understand that the crust of high civility covered deep fissures of social exploitation; that bourgeois sexual ethics were a veneer, masking a great area of turbulent hypocrisy; that the criteria of genuine literacy were applicable only to a few; that hatred between generations and classes ran deep, if often silent; that the safety of the *faubourg* and of the park was based squarely on the licensed but quarantined menace of the slum. Anyone who takes the trouble to find out will come to realize what a day's work was like in a Victorian factory, what infant mortality amounted to in the mining country of northern France in the 1870s and 80s. The recognition is inescapable that the intellectual wealth and stability of middle- and upper-middle-class life during the long liberal summer depended, directly, on economic and, ultimately military, dominion over vast portions of what is now known as the underdeveloped or third world. All this is manifest. We know it in our rational moments. Yet it is a kind of intermittent knowledge, less immediate to our pulse of feeling than is the mythology, the crystallized metaphor, at once generalized and compact, of a great garden of civility now ravaged.

In part, the nineteenth century itself is responsible for this nostalgic imagining. One can assemble from its own pronouncements an anthology of strenuous or complacent pride. The note of *Locksley Hall* can be heard at numerous moments and in different places. In Macaulay's famous encomium of the new horizon of science in the "Essay on Bacon" of 1837:

> It has lengthened life; it has mitigated pain; it has extinguished diseases; it has increased the fertility of the soil; it has given new securities to the mariner; it

has furnished new arms to the warrior; it has spanned
great rivers and estuaries with bridges of form unknown to our fathers; it has guided the thunderbolt
innocuously from the heaven to earth; it has lighted
up the night with the splendour of the day; it has extended the range of human vision; it has multiplied
the power of human muscles; it has accelerated motion; it has annihilated distance; it has facilitated intercourse, correspondence, all friendly offices, all dispatch
of business; it has enabled man to descend the depths
of the sea, to soar into the air, to penetrate securely into
the noxious recesses of the earth, to traverse the land
in cars which whirl along without horses, to cross the
ocean in ships which run ten knots an hour against the
wind. These are but a part of its fruits, and of its first-
fruits; for it is a philosophy which never rests, which
has never attained, which is never perfect. Its law is
progress.

The apotheosis at the close of *Faust* II, Hegelian historicism, with its doctrine of the self-realization of Spirit, the
positivism of Auguste Comte, the philosophic scientism of
Claude Bernard, are expressions of the same dynamic ser-
enity, of a trust in the unfolding excellence of fact. We
look back on these now with bewildered irony.

But other ages have made their boast. The image we
carry of a lost coherence, of a center that held, has authority
greater than historical truth. Facts can refute but not remove

it. It matches some profound psychological and moral need. It gives us poise, a dialectical counterweight with which to situate our own condition. This appears to be an almost organic, recursive process. Men of the Roman Empire looked back similarly on utopias of republican virtue; those who had known the *ancien régime* felt that their later years had fallen on an iron age. Circumstantial dreams underwrite present nightmares. I am not seeking to deny this process or to expound an "authentic vision" of the liberal past. I simply propose to look at the "summer of 1815-1915" from a somewhat different perspective—not as a symbolic whole whose contrasting virtues stand almost in indictment of our own difficulties, but as a source of those very difficulties. It is my thesis that certain specific origins of the inhuman, of the crises of our own time that compel a redefinition of culture, are to be found in the long peace of the nineteenth century and at the heart of the complex fabric of civilization.

The motif I want to fix on is that of *ennui*. "Boredom" is not an adequate translation, nor is *Langweile* except, perhaps, in Schopenhauer's usage; *la noia* comes much nearer. I have in mind manifold processes of frustration, of cumulative *désœuvrement*. Energies eroded to routine as entropy increases. Repeated motion or inactivity, sufficiently prolonged, secrete a poison in the blood, an acid torpor. Febrile lethargy; the drowsy nausea (so precisely described by Coleridge in the *Biographia Literaria*) of a man who misses a step in a dark staircase—there are many approximate terms and images. Baudelaire's use of "spleen" comes closest: it conveys the kinship, the simultaneity of exasperated, vague waiting—but for what?—and of gray lassitude:

> Rien n'égale en longueur les boiteuses journées,
> Quand sous les lourds flocons des neigeuses années
> L'ennui, fruit de la morne incuriosité,
> Prend les proportions de l'immortalité.
> —Désormais tu n'es plus, ô matière vivante!
> Qu'un granit entouré d'une vague épouvante,
> Assoupi dans le fond d'un Sahara brumeux;
> Un vieux sphinx ignoré du monde insoucieux,
> Oublié sur la carte, et dont l'humeur farouche
> Ne chante qu'aux rayons du soleil qui se couche. *
>
> > [*Les Fleurs du Mal* 76]

"Vague épouvante," "humeur farouche" are signals we shall want to keep in mind. What I want to stress here is the fact that a corrosive *ennui* is as much an element of nineteenth-century culture as was the dynamic optimism of the positivist and the Whig. It was not only, in Eliot's arresting

---

*Nothing is as interminable as those limping days / When, beneath the heavy flakes of snowbound years / Ennui, fruit of dreary apathy, / Takes on dimensions of everlastingness. / Henceforth, oh living form, you are nothing more / Than a block of granite surrounded by an aura of indistinct terror, / Drowsing in the deeps of a misty Sahara; / You are nothing more than an old sphinx disregarded by a careless world, / Forgot on the map, an old sphinx whose fierce temperament / Gives echoing reverberation only to the rays of the setting sun.

phrase, the souls of housemaids that were damp. A kind of marsh gas of boredom and vacuity thickened at crucial nerve-ends of social and intellectual life. For every text of Benthamite confidence, of proud meliorism, we can find a counterstatement of nervous fatigue. 1851 was the year of the Universal Exhibition, but also of the publication of a group of desolate, autumnal poems, which Baudelaire issued under the significant title *Les Limbes*. To me the most haunting, prophetic outcry of the nineteenth century is Théophile Gautier's "plutôt la barbarie que l'ennui!" If we can come to understand the sources of that perverse longing, of that itch for chaos, we will be nearer to an understanding of our own state and of the relations of our condition to the accusing ideal of the past.

No string of quotations, no statistics, can recapture for us what must have been the inner excitement, the passionate adventure of spirit and emotion unleashed by the events of 1789 and sustained, at a fantastic tempo, until 1815. Far more than political revolution and war, on an unprecedented scale of geographical and social compass, is involved. The French Revolution and the Napoleonic Wars—*la grande épopée*—literally quickened the pace of felt time. We lack histories of the internal time-sense, of the changing beat in men's experience of the rhythms of perception. But we do have reliable evidence that those who lived through the 1790s and the first decade and a half of the nineteenth century, and who could recall the tenor of life under the old dispensation, felt that time itself and the whole enterprise of consciousness had formidably accelerated. Kant's reputed lateness on his morning walk when news came of the fall of the Bastille, and the decision of the Republican régime to start the calendar of human affairs anew with *l'an un* are images of this great change. Even in the mind of contemporaries, each successive year of political struggle and social upheaval took on a distinct, graphic individuality. 1789, *Quatrevingt-treize*, 1812, are far more than temporal designations: they stand for great storms of being, for metamorphoses of the historical landscape so violent as to acquire, almost at once, the simplified magnitude of legend. (Because music is so immediately inwoven with changes in the shapes of time, the development of Beethoven's tempi, of the driving pulse in his symphonic and chamber music during the relevant years, is of extraordinary historical and psychological interest.)

Together with this accelerando, there occurred a "growing more dense" of human experience. The notion is difficult to set out abstractly. But it crowds on us, unmistakably, from contemporary literature and private record. The modern advertisement nostrum about "feeling more alive than before" had a literal force. Until the French Revolution and the marches and countermarches of the Napoleonic armies from Corunna to Moscow, from Cairo to Riga, history had been, very largely, the privilege and terror of the few. Certainly in respect of defined consciousness. All human beings were subject to general disaster or exploitation as they were to disease. But these swept over them with tidal

mystery. It is the events of 1789 to 1815 that interpenetrate
common, private existence with the perception of historical
processes. The *levée en masse* of the Revolutionary armies
was far more than an instrument of long-continued warfare
and social indoctrination. It did more than terminate the
old conventions of professional, limited warfare. As Goethe
noted acutely on the field at Valmy, populist armies, the
concept of a nation under arms, meant that history had become everyman's milieu. Henceforth, in Western culture,
each day was to bring news—a perpetuity of crisis, a break
with the pastoral silences and uniformities of the eighteenth
century made memorable in De Quincey's account of the
mails racing through England with news of the Peninsular
Wars. Wherever ordinary men and women looked across
the garden hedge, they saw bayonets passing. As Hegel
completed the *Phenomenology*, which is the master statement of the new density of being, he heard the hoofbeats
of Napoleon's escort passing through the nocturnal street
on the way to the battle of Jena.

We also lack a history of the future tense (in another
context I am trying to show what such a phenomenology of
internal grammar would be). But it is clear that the Revolutionary and Napoleonic decades brought on an overwhelming immanence, a deep, emotionally stressed change in the
quality of hope. Expectations of progress, of personal and
social enfranchisement, which had formerly had a conventional, often allegoric character, as of a millenary horizon,
suddenly moved very close. The great metaphor of renewal,

of the creation, as by a second coming of secular grace, of a just, rational city for man, took on the urgent drama of concrete possibility. The eternal "tomorrow" of utopian political vision became, as it were, Monday morning. We experience something of this dizzying sense of total possibility when reading the decrees of the *Convention* and of the Jacobin régime: injustice, superstition, poverty are to be eradicated *now*, in the next glorious hour. The world is to shed its worn skin a fortnight hence. In the grammar of Saint-Juste the future tense is never more than moments away. If we seek to trace this irruption—it was that violent —of dawn into private sensibility, we need look only to Wordsworth's *Prelude* and to the poetry of Shelley. The crowning statement, perhaps, is to be found in Marx's economic and political manuscripts of 1844. Not since early Christianity had men felt so near to renovation and to the end of night.

The quickening of time, the new vehemence and historicity of private consciousness, the sudden nearness of the messianic future contributed to a marked change in the tone of sexual relations. The evidence is plain enough. It comes as early as Wordsworth's "Lucy" poems and the penetrating remark on sexual appetite in the 1800 *Preface* to the *Lyrical Ballads*. It declares itself from a comparison, even cursory, between Swift's *Journal to Stella* and Keats's letters to Fanny Brawne. Nothing I know of at an earlier period truly resembles the self-dramatizing, self-castigating eroticism of Hazlitt's extraordinary *Liber Amoris* (1823).

Many elements are in play: the "sexualization" of the very landscape, making of weather, season, and the particular hour a symbolic restatement of the erotic mood; a compulsion to experience more intimately, to experience sex to the last pitch of nervous singularity, and at the same time to make this experience public. I can make out what must have been contributory causes: the partial emancipation of women and the actual role of a number of them in political life and argument; the breakdown of usages of decorum and formal reticence which had been a part of the caste system of the *ancien régime*. It is not difficult to see in what ways an intensification and widening of the erotic could be a counterpart to the dynamics of revolution and European conquest. Nevertheless, the phenomenon, with its culmination in Wagner's amalgam of eros and history, remains complicated and in certain regards obscure. The fact that our own sexuality is distinctly post-romantic, that many of of our own conventions stem directly from the revaluation of the erotic in the period from Rousseau to Heine, does not make analysis any simpler.

But taking these different strands together, one can say confidently that immense transmutations of value and perception took place in Europe over a time span more crowded, more sharply registered by individual and social sensibility, than any other of which we have reliable record. Hegel could argue, with rigorous logic of feeling, that history itself was passing into a new state of being, that ancient time was at an end.

What followed was, of course, a long spell of reaction and stasis. Depending on one's political idiom, one can see it either as a century of repression by a bourgeoisie that had turned the French Revolution and the Napoleonic extravaganza to its own economic advantage, or as a hundred years of liberal gradualism and civilized order. Broken only by convulsive but contained revolutionary spasms in 1830, 1848, and 1871, and by short wars of an intensely professional, socially conservative character, such as the Crimean and the Prussian Wars, this hundred years' peace shaped Western society and established the criteria of culture which have, until very recently, been ours.

To many who personally experienced the change, the drop in tension, the abrupt drawing of curtains against the morning, were deeply enervating. It is to the years after Waterloo that we must look for the roots of "the great *ennui*," which, as early as 1819, Schopenhauer defined as the corrosive illness of the new age.

What was a gifted man to do after Napoleon? How could organisms bred for the electric air of revolution and imperial epic breathe under the leaden sky of middle-class rule? How was it possible for a young man to hear his father's tales of the Terror and of Austerlitz and to amble down the placid boulevard to the countinghouse? The past drove rats' teeth into the gray pulp of the present; it exasperated, it sowed wild dreams. Of that exasperation comes a major literature. Musset's *La Confession d'un enfant du siècle* (1835-36) looks back with ironic *misère* on the start

of the great boredom. The generation of 1830 was damned
by memories of events, of hopes, in which it had taken no
personal part. It nursed within "un fonds d'incurable
tristesse et d'incurable ennui." No doubt there was nar-
cissism in this cultivation, the somber complacency of
dreamers who, from Goethe to Turgenev, sought to identify with Hamlet. But the void was real, and the sensation
of history gone absurdly wrong. Stendhal is the chronicler
of genius of this frustration. He had participated in the
insane vitality of the Napoleonic era; he conducted the rest
of his life in the ironic guise of a man betrayed. It is a
terrible thing to be "languissant d'ennui au plus beau
moment de la vie, de seize ans jusqu'à vingt" (Mlle. de La
Mole's condition before she resolves to love Julien Sorel in
Le Rouge et le noir). Madness, death are preferable to the
interminable Sunday and suet of a bourgeois life-form.
How can an intellectual bear to feel within himself something of Bonaparte's genius, something of that demonic
strength which led from obscurity to empire, and see before
him nothing but the tawdry flatness of bureaucracy? Raskol-
nikov writes his essay on Napoleon and goes out to kill an
old woman.

The collapse of revolutionary hopes after 1815, the brutal
deceleration of time and radical expectation, left a reservoir
of unused, turbulent energies. The romantic generation was
jealous of its fathers. The "antiheroes," the spleen-ridden
dandies in the world of Stendhal, Musset, Byron, and Push-
kin, move through the bourgeois city like condottieri out

of work. Or worse, like condottieri meagerly pensioned before their first battle. Moreover, the city itself, once festive with the tocsin of revolution, had become a prison.

For although politics had entered the phase of bland mendacity analyzed by Stendhal in *Lucien Leuwen*, the economic-industrial growth released by continental war and the centralized consciousness of the new nation-states took place exponentially. The "dark Satanic mills" were everywhere creating the soiled, hybrid landscape which we have inherited. The theme of alienation, so vital to any theory of the crisis of culture, is, as both Hegel and Saint-Simon were among the first to realize, directly related to the development of mass-manufacture. It is in the early and mid-nineteenth century that occur both the dehumanization of laboring men and women in the assembly-line system, and the dissociation between ordinary educated sensibility and the increasingly complex, technological artifacts of daily life. In manufacture and the money market, energies barred from revolutionary action or war could find outlet and social approval. Such expressions as "Napoleons of finance" and "captains of industry" are semantic markers of this modulation.

The immense growth of the monetary-industrial complex also brought with it the modern city, what a later poet was to call *la ville tentaculaire*—the megalopolis whose uncontrollable cellular division and spread now threatens to choke so much of our lives. Hence the definition of a new, major conflict: that between the individual and the stone sea that may, at any moment, overwhelm him. The urban inferno, with its hordes of faceless inhabitants, haunts the nine-teenth-century imagination. Sometimes the metropolis is a jungle, the crazed tropical growth of *Hard Times* and Brecht's *Im Dickicht der Stadt*. A man must make his mark on its indifferent immensity, or he will be cast off like the rags, the dawn flotsam which obsessed Baudelaire. In his invention of Rastignac, looking down on Paris, challenging the city to mortal combat, Balzac dramatized one of the focal points of the modern crisis. It is precisely from the 1830s onward that one can observe the emergence of a characteristic "counterdream"—the vision of the city laid waste, the fantasies of Scythian and Vandal invasion, the Mongol steeds slaking their thirst in the fountains of the Tuileries Gardens. An odd school of painting develops: pictures of London, Paris, or Berlin seen as colossal ruins, famous landmarks burnt, eviscerated, or located in a weird emptiness among charred stumps and dead water. Romantic fantasy anticipates Brecht's vengeful promise that nothing shall remain of the great cities except the wind that blows through them. Exactly a hundred years later, these apoca-lyptic collages and imaginary drawings of the end of Pom-peii were to be our photographs of Warsaw and Dresden. It needs no psychoanalysis to suggest how strong a part of wish-fulfillment there was in these nineteenth-century intimations.

The conjunction of extreme economic-technical dynam-ism with a large measure of enforced social immobility, a

conjunction on which a century of liberal, bourgeois civilization was built, made for an explosive mixture. It provoked
in the life of art and of intelligence certain specific, ultimately destructive ripostes. These, it seems to me, constitute
the meaning of Romanticism. It is from them that will grow
the nostalgia for disaster.

Here I am on familiar ground and can move rapidly.
In romantic pastoralism there is as much of a flight *from*
the devouring city as there is a return *to* nature. What needs
close attention is the extent to which critiques of urban
society tend to become indictments of all formal, complex
civilization as such ("civilization," of course, has in it
the word for city). Rousseauist naturalism has an obvious
destructive edge.

Romantic exoticism, that longing for *le pays lointain*, for
"faery lands forlorn," reflected different hurts: *ennui*, a
feeling of impotence in the face of political reaction and
philistine rule, a hunger for new colors, new shapes, new
possibilities of nervous discovery, to set against the morose
proprieties of bourgeois and Victorian modes. It also had
its strain of primitivism. If Western culture had gone bad
in the teeth, there might be sources of new vision among
distant savageries. Mallarmé's *Brise marine* concentrates
each of these elements into an ironic whole:

> La chair est triste, hélas! et j'ai lu tous les livres.
> Fuir! là-bas fuir! Je sens que des oiseaux sont ivres

D'être parmi l'écume inconnue et les cieux!
Rien, ni les vieux jardins reflétés par les yeux
Ne retiendra ce cœur qui dans la mer se trempe
O nuits! ni la clarté déserte de ma lampe
Sur le vide papier que la blancheur défend,
Et ni la jeune femme allaitant son enfant.
Je partirai! Steamer balançant ta mâture,
Lève l'ancre pour une exotique nature!
Un Ennui, désolé par les cruels espoirs,
Croit encore à l'adieu suprême des mouchoirs!*

Romantic ideals of love, notably the stress on incest, dramatize the belief that sexual extremism, the cultivation of the pathological, can restore personal existence to a full pitch of reality and somehow negate the gray world of middle-class fact. It is permissible to see in the Byronic theme of damnation through forbidden love and in the Wagnerian *Liebestod* surrogates for the lost dangers of revolutionary action.

The artist becomes hero. In a society made inert by repressive authority, the work of art becomes the quintessential deed. That is the claim put forward in Berlioz's *Benvenuto*

Flesh is sad, alas! and I have read all books. / To flee! To flee to that far place! I sense that the birds are joy-drunk finding themselves amid the unknown spume and skies! / Nothing, oh nights! shall hold back this heart, which soaks itself in the sea. / Neither the lone brightness of my desk lamp / Over the blank paper which a whiteness guards, / Nor the young woman nursing her child. / I shall leave! Steamer under your swinging masts and spars, / Raise anchor, bound towards an exotic world! / An Ennui, made desolate by cruel hopes, / Has faith still in the supreme adieu of waving handkerchiefs!

Cellini, in Zola's *l'Oeuvre*. Shelley went further. Though outwardly harried and powerless, the poet is "the unacknowledged legislator" of mankind. Or, as Victor Hugo proclaimed, he is *le Mage*, the divinely gifted necromancer in the van of human progress. It is not these propositions in themselves I want to consider, but only the degree of exasperation, of estrangement between society and the shaping forces of spirit which they betray.

All these currents of frustration, of illusory release, and of ironic defeat are registered, with unequaled precision, in the novels and private life of Flaubert. The figure of Emma Bovary incarnates, at a cruelly trivialized level, the roused and thwarted energies of dreams and desires for which mid-nineteenth-century society would allow no scope. *L'Education sentimentale* is the great "anti-*Bildungsroman*," the record of an education "away from" felt life and toward bourgeois torpor. *Bouvard et Pécuchet* is a long whine of loathing, of nausea at the apparently unshakable regimen of middle-class values. And there is *Salammbô*. Written almost exactly in mid-century, this frenetic yet congealed narrative of blood-lust, barbaric warfare, and orgiastic pain takes us to the heart of our problem. The sadism of the book, its scarcely governed ache for savagery, stem immediately from Flaubert's account of his own condition. Since adolescence, he had felt nothing but "insatiable desires" and "un ennui atroce."

Reading only these novels, one should have sensed much of the void that was undermining European stability. One should have known that *ennui* was breeding detailed fantasies of nearing catastrophe. Most of what has occurred since has its specific origins in the tensions of nineteenth-century society, in a complex of attitudes which, in hindsight, we think of too readily as a model for culture itself.

Ought one to go further? Is it reasonable to suppose that every high civilization will develop implosive stresses and impulses towards self-destruction? Does so delicately balanced, simultaneously dynamic and confined an aggregate as a complex culture tend, necessarily, towards a state of instability and, finally, of conflagration? The model would be that of a star which, after attaining a critical mass, a critical equation of energy exchanges between internal structure and radiant surface, will collapse inward, flaring out, at the moment of destruction, with just that magnitude of visible brilliance which we associate with great cultures in their terminal phase. Is the phenomenology of *ennui* and of a longing for violent dissolution a constant in the history of social and intellectual forms once they have passed a certain threshhold of complication?

I want to come back to this question at different points in my argument. To ask it at all is, of course, to follow on Freud's *Civilization and Its Discontents*, and to consider once again, the nihilist pastoralism of Rousseau. Freud's essay is itself a poetic construct, an attempt to devise a myth of reason with which to contain the terror of history. The notion of a death wish, operative in both individual and collective consciousness, is, as Freud himself emphasized, a philosophic trope. It goes frankly beyond the available psychological and sociological data. But the suggestion is of extraordinary force, and Freud's portrayal of the tensions which civilized manners impose on central, unfulfilled human instincts remains valid. As do the hints, abundant in psychoanalytic literature (which is itself post-Darwinian), that there is in human interrelations an inescapable drive towards war, towards a supreme assertion of identity at the cost of mutual destruction. Again, I want to return to these ideas. They are obviously cardinal to any contemporary theory of culture.

Whether the psychic mechanisms involved were universal or historically localized, one thing is plain: by ca. 1900 there was a terrible readiness, indeed a thirst for what Yeats was to call the "blood-dimmed tide." Outwardly brilliant and serene, *la belle époque* was menacingly overripe. Anarchic compulsions were coming to a critical pitch beneath the garden surface. Note the prophetic images of subterranean danger, of destructive agencies ready to rise from sewerage and cellar, that obsess the literary imagination from the time of Poe and *Les Misérables* to Henry James's *Princess Casamassima*. The arms race and the mounting fever of European nationalism were, I think, only the outward symptoms of this essential malaise. Intellect and feeling were, literally, fascinated by the prospect of a purging fire.

I. F. Clarke's *Voices Prophesying War* provides a lucid account of this fascination, of the anticipations of global conflict in poetry and fiction as they came to a head from the 1870s on. In all this mass of premonitory fantasy, only H. G. Wells's *World Set Free* was to prove wholly accurate. Written during 1913, it foresaw, with eerie precision, "the unquenchable crimson conflagrations of the atomic bombs." And even Wells could not prophesy the true measure of the dissolution of civilized norms, of human hopes, that was to come.

2 · *A Season in Hell*

The Viennese ironist Karl Kraus remarked that "on the matter of Hitler" nothing occurred to him— "es fällt mir nichts ein." How is one to address oneself, without a persistent feeling of fatuity, even of indecency, to the theme of ultimate inhumanity? Is there anything new to be said regarding the causes and forms of the breakdown of the European order in the "Thirty Years' War" from 1915 to 1945? Already the literature is too extensive and specialized for any single student to master. It comprises general and monographic material in history, economics, sociology, psychology, and intermediate disciplines. There have been important studies of mass behavior, of the totalitarian personality, of the relations between class conflict and world war. Nearly every facet of the Versailles settlement, of economic depression, of the concentration camp state has been investigated. How can one hope to contribute anything useful, particularly of a general, theoretic character?

Yet I think one must try. Large as it is, the literature remains, with very few exceptions, curiously inconclusive. The very business of rational analysis grows unsteady before the enormity of the facts. Consequently, there have been few attempts to relate the dominant phenomenon of twentieth-century barbarism to a more general theory of culture. Not very many have asked, or pressed home the question, as to the internal relations between the structures of the inhuman and the surrounding, contemporary matrix of high civilization. Yet the barbarism which we have undergone reflects, at numerous and precise points, the culture which it sprang from and set out to desecrate. Art, intellectual pursuits, the development of the natural sciences, many branches of scholarship flourished in close spatial, temporal proximity to massacre and the death camps. It is the structure and meaning of that proximity which must be looked at. Why did humanistic traditions and models of conduct prove so fragile a barrier against political bestiality? In fact, were they a barrier, or is it more realistic to perceive in humanistic culture express solicitations of authoritarian rule and cruelty?

I fail to see how any argument on the definition of culture, on the viability of the concept of moral values, can avoid these questions. A theory of culture, an analysis of our present circumstance, which do not have at their pivot a consideration of the modes of terror that brought on the death, through war, starvation, and deliberate massacre, of some seventy million human beings in Europe and Russia, between the start of the first World War and the end of the second, seem to me irresponsible.

But there is a second danger. Not only is the relevant material vast and intractable: it exercises a subtle, corrupting fascination. Bending too fixedly over hideousness, one feels queerly drawn. In some strange way the horror flatters attention, it gives to one's own limited means a spurious resonance. The last poems of Sylvia Plath are the classic locus of that temptation and vertigo. I am not sure whether anyone, however scrupulous, who spends time and imagin-

ative resources on these dark places can or, indeed, ought
to leave them personally intact. Yet the dark places are at
the center. Pass them by and there can be no serious discus-
sion of the human potential.

As we have seen, anticipations of war and fantasies of
universal destruction were rife. But with very few exceptions—such as Soloviev's vision of a new outpouring of
Asiatic hordes over Europe, or Péguy's solemn, uncannily
clairvoyant invocation of Armageddon in *Ève*—no one
foresaw the scale of slaughter. It is that numerical scale,
the daily inventory of death, which makes of 1915 the end
of the European order. Diplomatic and military historians
debate to this day whether there was not some appalling
miscalculation. What had turned professional, essentially
limited warfare into massacre? Different factors intervened:
the murderous solidification of the trenches, firepower, the
sheer area covered by the eastern and western fronts. But
there was also, one suspects, a matter of automatism: once
the elaborate machinery of conscription, transport, and
manufacture had slipped into gear, it became exceedingly
difficult to stop. The enterprise had its own logic outside
reason and human needs. In attacking the brute fact of
causality, of irreversible time and utilitarian process, the
Dada movement, as it sprang up in Zurich during the war
years, was in fact attacking the fabric of impotent rationality
which, every day, planned, authorized, justified the death
of tens of thousands.

And here, at once, a theory of culture faces a major difficulty. We are beginning to realize the extent and intricacy
of the genetic element in social history. But we have, even
now, only rudimentary means of gauging it. We know
something of the critical mass of genetic material and diversity needed to keep a civilization energized. We are beginning to understand a little more than we used to about
the nature of biological damage caused by such events as
the bubonic plagues of the fourteenth and seventeenth centuries, or by the depopulation of certain provinces of Germany and central Europe during the religious wars. But
our insights remain conjectural. What we can say, I think,
is this: the casualties of the first World War were not only
enormous, they were cruelly selective. It can, I believe, be
argued, with a good deal of supporting sociological and
demographic evidence, that the butcheries of Paschendael
and the Somme gutted a generation of English moral and
intellectual talent, that they eliminated many of the best
from the European future. The effects of the long massacre
on France were obviously profound, but more difficult to
assess. With the ravage of entire cadres and communities,
the close fabric of French life was thrown out of line. Much
of it has never recovered its equilibrium or elasticity.

We cannot think clearly about the crises of Western culture, about the origins and forms of totalitarian movements
in the European heartland and the recurrence of world war,
without bearing sharply in mind that Europe, after 1918,
was damaged in its centers of life. Decisive reserves of in-

telligence, of nervous resilience, of political talent, had been annihilated. The satiric conceit, in Brecht and Georges Grosz, of children murdered because never to be born has its specific genetic meaning. An aggregate of mental and physical potentiality, of new hybrids and variants, too manifold for us to measure, was lost to the preservation and further evolution of Western man and of his institutions. Already in a biological sense we are looking now at a diminished or "post-culture."

What had been miscalculation and uncontrollable mishap during the first World War became method during the second. In turning to the question of genocide, I must try and be as scrupulous, as skeptical as I am able to be, regarding my own motives. Much of my work has concerned itself, directly or indirectly, with trying to understand, to articulate, causal and teleological aspects of the holocaust. My own feelings are patently implicated. But so is the conviction that an analysis of the idea and ideal of culture demands the fullest possible understanding of the phenomenology of mass murder as it took place in Europe, from the Spanish south to the frontiers of Russian Asia between 1936 and 1945.

The failure of Eliot's *Notes towards a Definition of Culture* to face the issue, indeed to allude to it in anything but an oddly condescending footnote, is acutely disturbing. How, only three years after the event, after the publication to the world of facts and pictures that have, surely, altered our sense of the limits of human behavior, was it possible to write a book on culture and say nothing? How was it possible to detail and plead for a Christian order when the holocaust had put in question the very nature of Christianity and of its role in European history? Long-standing ambiguities on the theme of the Jew in Eliot's poetry and thought provide an explanation. But one is not left the less uncomfortable.

Yet in approaching the theme I find Eliot's insistence on the religious character of genuine civilization, and his "conception of culture and religion as being, when each term is taken in the right context, different aspects of the same thing," largely persuasive. It seems to me incontrovertible that the holocaust must be set in the framework of the psychology of religion, and that an understanding of this framework is vital to an argument on culture.

This is a minority view. Understandably, in an effort to make this insane material susceptible and bearable to reason, sociologists, economists, political scientists have striven to locate the topic in a rational, secular grid. They have investigated the opportunistic sources of Nazi racial theories; the long tradition of *petit-bourgeois* resentment against a seemingly aloof, prospering minority. They have pointed, rightly, to the psychological, symbolic links between inflationary collapse and the historical associations of Jewry and the money market. There have been penetrating studies of the imperfect, perhaps overhasty assimilation of secularized Jews into the gentile community, an assimilation which

produced much of the intellectual genius of modern Europe
but also, particularly in Germany, took on the guise of a
complex love-hate. Social historians have shown how numerous were the signs of developing hysteria between the
Dreyfus affair and the "final solution." Deliberate poisons
had been let loose. It has been argued, cogently, that there
is an ultimately rational, albeit murderous, motive behind
Nazi and Stalinist anti-Semitism: an attempt to get rid of
a minority whose inheritance and whose style of feeling
make of it a natural milieu for opposition, for potential
subversion.

Each of these lines of inquiry is important. Together they
make for an indispensable dossier of historical and sociological insight. But the phenomenon, so far as one is able
to take any coherent view of it at all, lies far deeper. No
historical or social-psychological model put forward until
now, no psychopathology of crowd behavior, of the psychic
infirmities of individual leaders and killers, no diagnosis of
planned hysteria accounts for certain salient features of the
problem. These include the active indifference—"active"
because "collaboratively unknowing"—of the vast majority
of the European population. They include the deliberate
decision of the National Socialist régime, even in the final
stages of economic warfare, to liquidate the Jews rather
than exploit them towards obvious productive and financial
ends. Most enigmatic of all, perhaps, is the persistence of
virulent anti-Semitism where no Jews or only a handful
survive (for example, in eastern Europe today). The mys-

tery, in the proper theological sense, is one of hatred without present object.

We are not, I believe, dealing with some monstrous accident in modern social history. The holocaust was not the
result of merely individual pathology or of the neuroses of
one nation-state. Indeed, competent observers expected the
cancer to spread first, and most virulently, in France. We
are not—and this is often misunderstood—considering
something truly analogous to other cases of massacre, to
the murder of the Gypsies or, earlier, of the Armenians.
There are parallels in technique and in the idiom of hatred.
But not ontologically, not at the level of philosophic intent.
That intent takes us to the heart of certain instabilities in
the fabric of Western culture, in the relations between instinctual and religious life. Hitler's jibe that "conscience
is a Jewish invention" provides a clue.

To speak of the "invention" of monotheism is to use
words in the most provisional way. The cast of intellect,
the social forms, the linguistic conventions which accompanied the change, it may be in the oasis at Kadesh, from
polytheism to the Mosaic concept of one God, are beyond
recall. We cannot feel our way into the minds and skins of
the men and women who, evidently under constraint and
amid frequent rebellion, passed into a new mapping of the
world. The immensity of the event, its occurrence in real
time, are certain, and reverberate still. But how the ancient
concretions of worship, the ancient, natural reflexes of

multitudinous animism were replaced, we have no way of knowing. The light curves towards us from across the remotest horizon. What we must recapture to mind, as nakedly as we can, is the singularity, the brain-hammering strangeness, of the monotheistic idea. Historians of religion tell us that the emergence of the concept of the Mosaic God is a unique fact in human experience, that a genuinely comparable notion sprang up at no other place or time. The abruptness of the Mosaic revelation, the finality of the creed at Sinai, tore up the human psyche by its most ancient roots. The break has never really knit.

The demands made of the mind are, like God's name, unspeakable. Brain and conscience are commanded to vest belief, obedience, love in an abstraction purer, more inaccessible to ordinary sense than is the highest of mathematics. The God of the Torah not only prohibits the making of images to represent Him. He does not allow imagining. His attributes are, as Schoenberg concisely expressed them in *Moses und Aron*,

> Unvorstellbar, weil unsichtbar;
> weil unüberblickbar;
> weil unendlich;
> weil ewig;
> weil allgegenwärtig;
> weil allmächtig.*

Inconceivable because invisible; / because immeasurable; / because everlasting; / because eternal; / because omnipresent; / because omnipotent.

No fiercer exigence has ever pressed on the human spirit, with its compulsive, organically determined bias towards image, towards figured presence. How many human beings have ever been capable, could be capable of, housing in themselves an inconceivable omnipresence? To all but a very few the Mosaic God has been from the outset, even when passionately invoked, an immeasurable Absence, or a metaphor modulating downward to the natural sphere of poetic, imagistic approximation. But the exaction stays in force—immense, relentless. It hammers at human consciousness, demanding that it transcend itself, that it reach out into a light of understanding so pure that it is itself blinding. We turn back into grossness and, what is more important, into self-reproach. Because the ideal is still there, because, in Blake's shorthand for the tyranny of the revealed, light presses on the brain. In polytheism, says Nietzsche, lay the freedom of the human spirit, its creative multiplicity. The doctrine of a single Deity, whom men cannot play off against other gods and thus win open spaces for their own aims, is "the most monstrous of all human errors" ("die ungeheuerlichste aller menschlichen Verirrungen").

In his late work *Moses and Monotheism* Freud ascribed the commission of this "error" to an Egyptian prince and seer of the scattered house of Ikhnaton. Many have wondered why he should have sought to shift from his own people that supreme weight of glory. Freud himself seems to have been unaware of the motive. It will, I hope, emerge from my argument.

Historically, the requirements of absolute monotheism proved all but intolerable. The Old Testament is a record of mutiny, of spasmodic but repeated reversions to the old gods, whom the hand can touch and the imagination house. Pauline Christianity found a useful solution. While retaining something of the idiom and centralized symbolic lineaments of monotheism, it allowed scope for the pluralistic, pictorial needs of the psyche. Be it in their Trinitarian aspects, in their proliferation of saintly and angelic persons, or in their vividly material realization of God the Father, of Christ, of Mary, the Christian churches have, with very rare exceptions, been a hybrid of monotheistic ideals and polytheistic practices. That has been their suppleness and syncretic strength. The single, unimaginable—rigorously speaking, "unthinkable"—God of the Decalogue has nothing to do with the threefold, thoroughly visualized pantheon of the churches.

But that God, blank as the desert air, would not rest. The memory of His ultimatum, the presence of His Absence, have goaded Western man. The nineteenth century thought it had laid the great specter to rest. The canonic text is Nietzsche's monologue of the madman in *La Gaia Scienza*. The words are so overwhelming, they are so near the heart of the being of man today, that I want to quote in full, and in the original language:

Wohin ist Gott? rief er, ich will es euch sagen! Wir
haben ihn getötet—ihr und ich! Wir alle sind seine
Mörder! Aber wie haben wir dies gemacht? Wie ver-
mochten wir das Meer auszutrinken? Wer gab uns den
Schwamm, um den ganzen Horizont wegzuwischen?
Was taten wir, als wir diese Erde von ihrer Sonne
losketteten? Wohin bewegt sie sich nun? Wohin be-
wegen wir uns? Fort von allen Sonnen? Stürzen wir
nicht fortwährend? Und rückwärts, seitwärts, vorwärts
nach allen Seiten? Gibt es noch ein Oben und ein
Unten? Irren wir nicht wie durch ein unendliches
Nichts? Haucht uns nicht der leere Raum an? Ist es
nicht kälter geworden? Kommt nicht immerfort die
Nacht und mehr Nacht? Müssen nicht Laternen am
Vormittage angezündet werden? Hören wir noch
nichts von dem Lärm der Totengräber, welche Gott
begraben? Riechen wir noch nichts von der göttlichen
Verwesung?—auch Götter verwesen! Gott ist tot! Gott
bleibt tot! Und wir haben ihn getötet! Wie trösten wir
uns, die Mörder aller Mörder? Das Heiligste und
Mächtigste, was die Welt bisher besass, es ist unter
unseren Mesern verblutet—we wischt dies Blut von
uns ab?*

---

*"Whereto has God gone?" he cried. I shall tell you! "We have slain him
—you and I! All of us are his murderers! But how have we done this?
How had we the means to drink the sea dry? Who gave us a sponge to
efface the entire horizon? What were we about when we uncoupled this
earth from its sun? Where is the earth moving to now? Where are we
moving? Away from all suns? Are we falling continuously? And backward and sideways and forward in all directions? Is there still an above

But that deed was not enough. Only a psychologist of Nietzsche's genius and vulnerability could experience the "murder of God" directly, could feel at his own nerve-ends its liberating doom. There was an easier vengeance to hand, a simpler way of making good the centuries of *mauvaise foi*, of subconscious but aching resentment against the unattainable ideal of the one God. By killing the Jews, Western culture would eradicate those who had "invented" God, who had, however imperfectly, however restively, been the declarers of His unbearable Absence. The holocaust is a reflex, the more complete for being long-inhibited, of natural sensory consciousness, of instinctual polytheistic and animist needs. It speaks for a world both older than Sinai and newer than Nietzsche. When, during the first years of Nazi rule, Freud sought to shift to an Egyptian responsibility for the "invention" of God, he was, though perhaps without fully knowing it, making a desperate propitiatory, sacrificial move. He was trying to wrench the lightning rod out of the hands of the Jewish people. It was too late. The leprosy of God's choice— but who chose whom?—was too visible on them.

---

and a below? Are we not wandering lost as through an unending void? Does vacant space not breathe at us? Has it not grown colder? Is there not perpetual nightfall and more night? Must we not light lanterns in the morning? Do we hear nothing of the noise of the gravediggers who are burying God? Is there no smell of divine putrefaction?—the gods also decompose! God is dead! God stays dead! And we have killed him! How shall we comfort ourselves, who are killers above all killers? The holiest and mightiest that the world had hitherto possessed has bled to death under our knives—who shall wipe that blood off us?"

But the provocation was more than metaphysical. More than "a supreme fiction" of reason was being thrust on mulish humanity. The Books of the Prophets and the Sermon on the Mount and parables of Jesus which are so closely related to the prophetic idiom, constitute an unequaled act of moral demand. Because the words are so familiar, yet too great for ready use, we tend to forget or merely conventionalize the extremity of their call. Only he who loses his life, in the fullest sense of sacrificial self-denial, shall find life. The kingdom is for the naked, for those who have willingly stripped themselves of every belonging, of every sheltering egoism. There is no salvation in the middle places. For the true disciple of the prophets and of Jesus, the utmost ethical commitment is like common breath. To become man, man must make himself new, and in so doing stifle the elemental desires, weaknesses, and claims of the ego. Only he who can say with Pascal, "le moi est haissable," has even begun to obey the Gospels' altruistic imperative.

That imperative was stated and restated innumerable times in the course of Western history. It is the staple of Christian ethics, of the Christian doctrine of right living. How many could hope to respond adequately? In how many human careers were these prescripts of ascetic love, of compassion, of self-suppression, more than a Sunday tag? Apologetics of practical life, the prodigal economics of repentance, and "a fresh start," papered over the deep cracks between secular existence and the eschatological demand.

But the cracks would not mend. They opened explosively in the individual conscience (of Pascal, of Kierkegaard, of Dostoevski). By their simple presence, at every occasion of Christian worship, these fantastic moral requirements mock and undermine mundane values. They set anarchic love against reason, an end of time against history.

The result of this incessant dialectic was a profound unbalance at the pivot of Western culture, a corrosive pressure on the subconscious. Once again, as with abstract monotheism, men had enforced upon them ideals, norms of conduct, out of all natural grasp. And again, these challenges to perfection continued to weigh on individual lives, on social systems, in which they could not be honestly met.

The third confrontation between exigent utopia and the common pulse of Western life occurs with the rise of messianic socialism. Even where it proclaims itself to be atheist, the socialism of Marx, of Trotsky, of Ernst Bloch, is directly rooted in messianic eschatology. Nothing is more religious, nothing is closer to the ecstatic rage for justice in the prophets, than the socialist vision of the destruction of the bourgeois Gomorrah and the creation of a new, clean city for man. In their very language Marx's 1844 manuscripts are steeped in the tradition of messianic promise. In an astounding passage Marx seems to paraphrase the vision of Isaiah and of primitive Christianity: "Assume *man* to be *man* and his relationship to the world to be a human one: then you can exchange love only for love, trust for trust." When human exploitation is eradicated, the grime shall be scoured from the tired earth, and the world made a garden once more. This is the socialist dream and millenary bargain. For it generations have died. In its name falsehood and oppression have spread over a good deal of the earth. But the dream remains magnetic. It cries out to man to renounce profit and selfishness, to melt his personal being into that of the community. It demands that he break down the blackened walls of history, that he leap out of the shadow of his petty needs. Those who resist the dream are not only madmen and enemies of society; they betray the part of light in their own humanity. The god of utopia is a jealous god.

Monotheism at Sinai, primitive Christianity, messianic socialism: these are the three supreme moments in which Western culture is presented with what Ibsen termed "the claims of the ideal." These are the three stages, profoundly interrelated, through which Western consciousness is forced to experience the blackmail of transcendence. "Surmount yourself. Surpass the opaque barriers of the mind to attain pure abstraction. Lose your life in order to gain it. Give up property, rank, wordly comfort. Love your neighbor as you do yourself—no, much more, for self-love is sin. Make any sacrifice, endure any insult, even self-denunciation, so that justice may prevail." Unceasingly, the blackmail of perfection has hammered at the confused, mundane, egotistical fabric of common, instinctual behavior. Like a shrilling note in the inner ear. Men are neither saints nor ascetics; their imaginings are gross; ordinarily, their sense of the future is the next milestone. But the insistence of the ideal continued, with a terrible, tactless force.

Three times it sounded from the same historical center. (Some political scientists put at roughly 80 percent the proportion of Jews in the ideological development of messianic socialism and communism.) Three times, Judaism produced a summons to perfection and sought to impose it on the current and currency of Western life. Deep loathing built up in the social subconscious, murderous resentments. The mechanism is simple but primordial. *We hate most those who hold out to us a goal, an ideal, a visionary promise which, even though we have stretched our muscles to the utmost, we cannot reach, which slips, again and again, just out of range of our racked fingers—yet, and this is crucial, which remains profoundly desirable, which we cannot reject because we fully acknowledge its supreme value.* In his exasperating "strangeness," in his acceptance of suffering as part of a covenant with the absolute, the Jew became, as it were, the "bad conscience" of Western history. In him the abandonments of spiritual and moral perfection, the hypocrisies of an established, mundane religiosity, the Absences of a disappointed, potentially vengeful God, were kept alive and visible.

When it turned on the Jew, Christianity and European civilization turned on the incarnation—albeit an incarnation often wayward and unaware—of its own best hopes. It is something like this that Kafka meant in his arrogant humble assertion that "he who strikes a Jew strikes down man/mankind" (*den Menschen*). In the holocaust there was both a lunatic retribution, a lashing out against intolerable pressures of vision, and a large measure of self-mutilation. The secular, materialist, warlike community of modern Europe sought to extirpate from itself, from its own inheritance, archaic, now ridiculously obsolete, but somehow inextinguishable carriers of the ideal. In the Nazi idiom of "vermin" and "sanitation" there is a brusque insight into the infectious nature of morality. Kill the remembrancer, the claim agent, and you will have canceled the long debt.

The genocide that took place in Europe and the Soviet Union during the period 1936-45 (Soviet anti-Semitism being perhaps the most paradoxical expression of the hatred which reality feels towards failed utopia) was far more than a political tactic, an eruption of lower-middle-class malaise, or a product of declining capitalism. It was no mere secular, socioeconomic phenomenon. It enacted a suicidal impulse in Western civilization. It was an attempt to level the future—or, more precisely, to make history commensurate with the natural savageries, intellectual torpor, and material instincts of unextended man. Using theological metaphors, and there is no need to apologize for them in an essay on culture, the holocaust may be said to mark a second Fall. We can interpret it as a voluntary exit from the Garden and a programmatic attempt to burn the Garden behind us. Lest its remembrance continue to infect the health of barbarism with debilitating dreams or with remorse.

With the botched attempt to kill God and the very nearly

successful attempt to kill those who had "invented" Him, civilization entered, precisely as Nietzsche had foretold, "on night and more night."

By the mid-1760s, after the *affaire Calas*, Voltaire and his informed contemporaries expressed the confident belief that torture and other bestialities practiced on subjects or enemies were passing forever from civilized society. Like the Black Death and the burning of witches, these somber atavisms from primitive and prerational ages would not survive the new temper of European enlightenment. Secularization was the key. Torture and the annihilation of human communities, argued the *philosophes*, sprang directly from religious dogmatism. By proclaiming individuals or entire societies to be damned, by treating their convictions as pestilential heresies, church and state had deliberately loosed fanaticism and savagery on often helpless men. With the decline in the strength of religious creeds, there would follow, said Voltaire, a concomittant decline in human hatreds, in the urge to destroy another man because he is the embodiment of evil or falsehood. Indifference would breed tolerance.

Today, exactly two hundred years later, we find ourselves in a culture in which the methodical use of torture towards political ends is widely established. We come immediately after a stage of history in which millions of men, women, and children were made to ash. Currently, in different parts of the earth, communities are again being incinerated, tortured, deported. There is hardly a methodology of abjection and of pain which is not being applied somewhere, at this moment, to individuals and groups of human beings. Asked why he was seeking to arouse the whole of Europe over the judicial torture of one man, Voltaire answered, in March 1762, "c'est que je suis homme." By that token, he would, today, be in constant and vain cry.

That this should be the case is catastrophic. The wide-scale reversion to torture and mass murder, the ubiquitous use of hunger and imprisonment as political means · mark not only a crisis of culture but, quite conceivably, an abandonment of the rational order of man. It may well be that it is a mere fatuity, an indecency to debate of the definition of culture in the age of the gas oven, of the arctic camps, of napalm. The topic may belong solely to the past history of hope. But we should not take this contingency to be a natural fact of life, a platitude. We must keep in sharp focus its hideous novelty or renovation. We must keep vital in ourselves a sense of scandal so overwhelming that it affects every significant aspect of our position in history and society. We have, as Emily Dickinson would have said, to keep the soul terribly surprised. I cannot stress this enough. To Voltaire and Diderot the bestial climate of our national and social conflicts would have seemed a lunatic return to barbarism. To most intelligent men and women of the nineteenth century a prediction that torture and massacre were soon to be endemic again in "civilized" Europe would have seemed a nightmarish joke. There is nothing *natural* about our present condition. There is no self-evident logic or dignity in our current knowledge that "anything is possible." In fact, such knowledge corrupts and lowers the threshold of outrage (only Kierkegaard foresaw both the inchoate possibility and the corruption). The numb prodigality of our acquaintance with horror is a radical human defeat.

How did this defeat come about? The subject is not only an ugly one; it bristles with philosophic traps.

Precisely at the time when Voltaire was voicing his trust in the progress of justice and of humane power relations, a uniquely consequent program of terror was also being devised. So much pretentious nonsense has been written about Sade in the past twenty years by philosophers, psychologists, and critics—such writing being itself symptomatic—that one hesitates to revert to the theme. Anyone who has tried to read Sade will know that the material is of maniacal monotony; one gags on it. But that automatism, that crazed repetitiveness, has its importance. It directs us to a novel and particular image, or rather silhouette, of the human person. It is in Sade, as in certain details of Hogarth, that we find the first methodical industrialization of the human body. The tortures, the unnatural shapes, enforced on the victims of *Justine* and the *Cent-vingt jours*, represent, with consummate logic, an assembly-line and piecework model of human relations. Each limb, each nerve, is torn or twisted in turn, with the impartial, cold frenzy of the piston, the steam hammer, and the pneumatic drill. Each part of the body is seen only as a part and replaceable by "spares." In the pluralistic simultaneities of Sadian sexual assaults, we have a brilliantly exact *figura* of the division of labor on the factory floor. Sade's own suggestions that his palaces of pleasure are really laboratories, that every torment and humiliation will follow axiomatically from the perception of flesh as raw material, are cogent.

Thus there *are* links—both Engels and Ruskin were in no doubt on the issue—between mass manufacture, as it evolves in the late eighteenth and nineteenth centuries, and a movement towards dehumanization. Watching exhausted, brutalized factory workers pour into the street, Engels saw that a reservoir of subhuman impulses was filling. There is, doubtless, a sense in which the concentration camp reproduces the life-forms of the factory, in which the "final solution" is the application to human beings of warehouse and assembly-line techniques. Blake's vision of the "dark mills," which is contemporary with Sade, carried a precise charge of prophecy.

Yet the analogy is too simple. Apart from sporadic episodes of rational maltreatment, the death camps, like the Gothic keeps of *Justine*, are rigorously inefficient and counterproductive. Their deliberate product is waste. No industrial process could operate in that way. The new barbarism has adopted the instrumentalities of the industrial revolution. It has translated into human terms key aspects of the technology of materials. But its sources must be looked for at a deeper level.

It may be that the dramatic increase in the density of population in the new industrial-urban milieu is relevant. We conduct a good part of our lives amid the menacing jostle of the crowd. Enormous pressures of competing numbers build up against our needs of space, of privacy. The result is a contradictory impulse towards "clearance." On the one hand, the palpable mass of uniform life, the insect immensity of the city or beach crowd, devalues any sense of individual worth. It wholly deflates the mystery of the irreplaceable presence. On the other hand, and because our own identity is threatened by the smothering mass of the anonymous, we suffer destructive spasms, a blind need to lunge out and make room. Elias Canetti has made the intriguing suggestion that the ease of the holocaust relates to the collapse of currency in the 1920s. Large numbers lost all but a vaguely sinister, unreal meaning. Having seen a hundred thousand, then a million, then a billion Mark needed to buy bread or pay for bus tickets, ordinary men lost all perception of concrete enormity. The same large numbers tainted with unreality the disappearance and liquidation of peoples. There is evidence that men and women are only imperfectly adapted to coexist in the stifling proximity of the industrial-urban hive. Accumulating over a century, the increase in noise levels, in the pace of work and motion, in the intensity of artificial lighting, may have reached a pathological limit and triggered instincts of devastation.

It is, surely, notable that the theory of personality, as it develops from Hegel to Nietzsche and Freud (in many regards, Nietzsche's truest disciple), is essentially a theory of aggression. Hegel defines identity *against* the identity of others. Where it is ontologically realized, consciousness of the full self will implicate the subjection, perhaps the destruction, of another. All recognition is agonistic. We name our own being, as the Angel did Jacob, after the dialectic of mutual aggression. Nor is there anything in the analysis of human relations starker than the account of libido as narcissistic excess which Freud put forward in the pivotal year 1914. Love is fundamentally self-love, and the libido does not wish to go beyond the bounds of the inner self. It "detaches itself from the self, it aims itself on things outside," only when it is too full—again a phenomenology of crowding—when the richness of internalized consciousness threatens to break down the structure of the ego. The key sentence is, as often in Freud, of implacable grimness: "endlich muss man beginnen zu lieben, um nicht krank zu werden." But just because love is a forced remedy, because the primary thrust of the libido is towards ingestion of all realities into the self, there runs through human relations a drive towards the pulverization of the rival persona.

Thus there may be in the genocidal reflexes of the twentieth century, in the compulsive scale of massacre, a lashing out of the choked psyche, an attempt to "get air," to break the live prison-walls of an intolerably thronged condition.

Even at the price of ruin. The void quiet of the city after the fire storm, the emptiness of the field after the mass murder, may speak to some obscure but primal need for free space, for the silence in which the ego can cry out its mastery.

But valuable as they may be, these lines of conjecture do not, I think, lead to the center. It is to the ambiguous afterlife of religious feeling in Western culture that we must look, to the malignant energies released by the decay of natural religious forms.

We know from the plans of those who built them and from the testimony of inmates, that the death camps constituted a complete, coherent world. They had their own measure of time, which is pain. The unbearable was parceled out with pedantic nicety. The obscenities and abjections practiced in them were accompanied by prescribed rituals of derision and false promise. There were regulated gradations of horror within the total, concentric sphere. *L'univers concentrationnaire* has no true counterpart in the secular mode. Its analogue is Hell. The camp embodies, often down to minutiae, the images and chronicles of Hell in European art and thought from the twelfth to the eighteenth centuries. It is these representations which gave to the deranged horrors of Belsen a kind of "expected logic." The material realities of the inhuman are detailed, endlessly, in Western iconography, from the mosaics at Torcello to the panels of Bosch; they are prepared for from the fourteenth-century Harrowings of Hell to *Faust*. It is in the fantasies of the infernal, as they literally haunt Western sensibility, that we find the technology of pain without meaning, of bestiality without end, of gratuitous terror. For six hundred years the imagination dwelt on the flaying, the racking, the mockery of the damned, in a place of whips and hellhounds, of ovens and stinking air.

The literature of the camps is extensive. But nothing in it equals the fullness of Dante's observations. Having no personal experience of the *Arschloch der Welt*—that hideously exact and allegoric German term for Auschwitz and Treblinka—I can make only approximate sense of many of Dante's notations. But whoever can grasp, in canto 33 of the *Inferno*, the full meaning of "The very weeping there forbids to weep,"

> Lo pianto stesso li pianger non lascia,
>   e'l duol che truova in sugli occhi rintoppo,
>   si volge in entro a far crescer l'ambascia*

will, I believe, have grasped the ontological form of the camp world. The concentration and death camps of the twentieth century, wherever they exist, under whatever régime, are *Hell made immanent*. They are the transference of Hell from below the earth to its surface. They are the deliberate enactment of a long, precise imagining. Because it imagined more fully than any other text, because it argued the centrality of Hell in the Western order, the

---

The very weeping there forbids to weep, / And grief finding eyes blocked with tears / Turns inward to make agony greater.

Commedia remains our literal guidebook—to the flames, to the ice fields, to the meat hooks. In the camps the millenary pornography of fear and vengeance cultivated in the Western mind by Christian doctrines of damnation was realized.

Two centuries after Voltaire, and at a time when these doctrines had all but vanished into picturesque formality? This is the point. Much has been said of man's bewilderment and solitude after the disappearance of Heaven from active belief. We know of the neutral emptiness of the skies and of the terrors it has brought. But it may be that the loss of Hell is the more severe dislocation. It may be that the mutation of Hell into metaphor left a formidable gap in the coordinates of location, of psychological recognition in the Western mind. The absence of the familiar damned opened a vortex which the modern totalitarian state filled. To have neither Heaven nor Hell is to be intolerably deprived and alone in a world gone flat. Of the two, Hell proved the easier to re-create. (The pictures had always been more detailed.)

In our current barbarism an extinct theology is at work, a body of transcendent reference whose slow, incomplete death has produced surrogate, parodistic forms. The epilogue to belief, the passage of religious belief into hollow convention, seems to be a more dangerous process than the *philosophes* anticipated. The structures of decay are toxic. Needing Hell, we have learned how to build and run it on earth. A few miles from Goethe's Weimar or on the isles of Greece. No skill holds greater menace. Because we have it and are using it on ourselves, we are now in a *post-culture*. In locating Hell above ground, we have passed out of the major order and symmetries of Western civilization.

3 · In a Post-Culture

F irst, we must make what inventory we can of the irreparable. Psychologically, this is not an easy job. The physical, economic renascence of so much of Europe has been prodigious. Many cities are more handsome and populous than they were before devastation. The marks on the actual landscape made by World War I, the broken plateaus, the gouged fields, bit deeper than the traces left by 1940-45. Today, one can travel through most of western Europe, and even the Soviet Union, and find no precise ground on which to locate the facts of the second World War or one's own recollection of the ash hills of 1945. It is as if a violent instinct of effacement and renewal had prevailed, a creative amnesia. It was indecent to survive, let alone prosper again, in the graphic presence of the immediate past. Frequently, in fact, it was the totality of destruction which made possible the installation of entirely modern industrial plants. The German economic miracle is ironically but exactly proportionate to the extent of ruin in the Reich.

Yet the mechanized, often antiseptic landscape of contemporary Europe can be illusory. The new facades, crowded, economically dynamic as may be the spaces behind them, speak a curious emptiness. The test case lies in the restored urban centers. At great pains and cost, *Altstädtte*, whole cities, have been rebuilt, stone by numbered stone, geranium pot by geranium pot. Photographically there is no way of telling; the patina on the gables is even richer than before. But there is something unmistakably amiss. Go to Dresden or Warsaw, stand in one of the exquisitely recomposed squares in Verona, and you will feel it. The perfection of renewal has a lacquered depth. As if the light at the cornices had not been restored, as if the air were inappropriate and carried still an edge of fire. There is nothing mystical to this impression; it is almost painfully literal. It may be that the coherence of an ancient thing is harmonic with time, that the perspective of a street, of a roof line, that have lived their natural being can be replicated but not re-created (even where it is, ideally, indistinguishable from the original, reproduction is not the vital form). Handsome as it is, the Old City of Warsaw is a stage set; walking through it, the living create no active resonance. It is the image of those precisely restored house fronts, of those managed lights and shadows which I keep in mind when trying to discriminate between what is irretrievable—though it may still be about—and what has in it the pressure of life.

I have to leave out the genetic aspect, and this omission may be severely damaging. Obviously, our current state reflects formidable losses not only of human means—the individuals who would now be feeling and thinking with us—but also of future potentiality. Certain vital futures have been eliminated forever from the spectrum of possibility. But, as I said earlier, "biosociology" and historical genetics are, as yet, too rudimentary, too broad in their conceptual schemes, to allow any responsible, verifiable estimate of what the physiological impairment to Western civilization has been. What I want to consider is the destruction of inner forms.

The first of these involves the locale of high civilization. Western culture worked on the assumption, often unexamined, that its own legacy, the repertoire of its identifying recognitions, was in fact "the best that has been said and thought." Out of Judaeo-Hellenic sources, in a geography singularly tempered to creative man, in a racial matrix indistinctly but confidently felt to be preeminent, Western history had developed its privileged strength of being. Seen from that commanding nub, the histories, the social lives, the artistic and intellectual artifacts of other races and terrains took on a diminished, occasional air. Not that they were altogether ignored. At different times, Islamic and Far Eastern cultures impinged on the European sensibility. Eighteenth-century *chinoiserie*, the interest shown by certain Victorian thinkers and by the German idealist tradition in "the light from the East" are characteristic moments. But in neither case was there a feeling of genuine parity, let alone inferiority. The myth of the noble savage had interiorized a powerful hierarchic dogma: Western sensibility could dwell with nostalgic admiration on Oceanic virtues, and even see in such virtues a reproach to its own failings, precisely because its own primacy was not in serious question. Both the pastoral nostalgia and the self-criticism derived from a stable fulcrum.

That stability was not seriously undermined until the 1920s and 30s. The charismatic appeal of "barbaric forms" on the plastic and musical imagination, as occurs in jazz, in *Fauve* art, in dance, in the new theatre of masque and ritual, drew on several complex strains. But it cannot be dissociated from the catastrophe of world war and the sudden void of classic values. The African masks which grimace out of post-Cubic art are borrowings of and for despair. But even these explosive insinuations from without did not negate the Western inheritance. The latter continued to provide touchstones of order and of that unbroken continuum of intellectual power which had, in plain fact, made European and Anglo-Saxon man very largely master of the globe.

Today, after only a generation of crisis, this picture looks antiquarian. Slogan-mongers and pseudophilosophers have familiarized the West with the notion that the white man has been a leprosy on the skin of the earth, that his civilization is a monstrous imposture or, at best, a cruel, cunning disguise for economic, military exploitation. We are told, in tones of punitive hysteria, either that our culture is doomed—this being the Spenglerian model of rational apocalypse—or that it can be resuscitated only through a violent transfusion of those energies, of those styles of feeling, most representative of "third-world" peoples. Theirs is true "soul," theirs the beauty of blackness and of eros. This neoprimitivism (or penitential masochism) has roots in the core of the Western crisis and needs to be understood both psychologically and sociologically. I will come back to the question. The point to make is an obvious one: there can be no natural return to the lost centrality. For the great majority of thinking beings, certainly for the young, the image of Western culture as self-evidently superior, as embodying within itself almost the sum total of intellectual and moral power, is either a racially tinged absurdity or a museum piece. In America particularly—and America is, today, the main generator and storehouse of cultural means —the confident pivot of a classic geography is irreparably broken.

To what extent are that sense of loss and attendant guilt justified?

Contrary to the "Scythian" fantasies of nineteenth-century apocalyptic fables, barbarism did come from the European heartland. Though in parodistic and ultimately negating forms, political bestiality did take on certain of the conventions, idiom, and external values of high culture. And, as we have seen, the infection was, in numerous instances, reciprocal. Mined by *ennui* and the aesthetics of violence, a fair proportion of the intelligentsia and of the institutions of European civilization—letters, the academy, the performing arts—met inhumanity with varying degrees of welcome. Nothing in the next-door world of Dachau impinged on the great winter cycle of Beethoven chamber music played in Munich. No canvases came off the museum walls as the butchers strolled reverently past, guidebook in hand.

It is equally true that—to an extent as yet to be gauged by economic and social historians—many of the superflu-

ities, zones of leisure, and hierarchies implicit in Western
culture drew on the subjugation of other races and contin-
ents. That fact is not eradicated, only qualified, by the undoubted elements of creative exchange and beneficial
import in colonialism. Specific and often indefensible power
relations with and towards the rest of the world energized
the cultural predominance of the West. But to be seen in
its full scope, the indictment must also be internalized:
within classical and European civilization itself, numerous
representative achievements—literary, artistic, philosophic
—are inseparable from the milieu of absolutism, of extreme
social injustice, even of gross violence, in which they flourished. To be argued seriously, the question of "the guilt
of civilization" must include not only colonialism and the
rapacities of empire but the true nature of the relations
between the production of great art and thought, on the
one hand, and of régimes of violent and repressive order,
on the other. In short, it is an argument that involves not
only the white man's rule in Africa or India but, each in
its own way, the Medicean court, Racine at Versailles, and
the current genius of Russian literature. (In what sense is
Stalinism the necessary condition for a Mandelstam, a Pas-
ternak, a Solzhenitsyn?)

But however accusingly, with whatever penitential hysteria, the argument is put, the fact of Western dominance
during two and a half millennia remains largely true. *Pace*
Joseph Needham, whose reorientation of the cultural and
scientific map in favor of China and, possibly, India, is

itself among the most fascinating, imaginative of modern *Western* intellectual adventures, the manifest centers of philosophic, scientific, poetic force have been situated within the Mediterranean, north European, Anglo-Saxon racial and geographic matrix. The causes for this hegemony are obviously manifold and, very likely, too complexly interactive for any single intelligence or theory of history to analyze. They may range from considerations of climate and nutrition (the high levels of protein available to Western communities), the whole way to those minute collocations of genetic inheritance and accident about whose shaping role in history we know so little. But it remains a truism—or ought to—that the world of Plato is not that of the shamans, that Galilean and Newtonian physics have made a major portion of human reality articulate to the mind, that the inventions of Mozart reach beyond drum-taps and Javanese bells—moving, heavy with remembrance of other dreams as these are. And it is true also that the very posture of self-indictment, of remorse in which much of educated Western sensibility now finds itself, is again a culturally specific phenomenon. What other races have turned in penitence to those whom they once enslaved, what other civilizations have morally indicted the brilliance of their own past? The reflex of self-scrutiny in the name of ethical absolutes is, once more, a characteristically Western, post-Voltairian act.

Our current incapacity to state these obvious points openly, to coexist with them outside a network of guilt and masochistic impulse, poses severe problems. Seeking to placate the furies of the present, we demean the past. We soil that legacy of eminence which, whatever our personal limitations, we are invited to take part in, by our history, by our Western languages, by the carapace and, if you will, burden of our skins. The evasions, moreover, the self-denials and arbitrary restructurings of historical remembrance which guilt forces on us, are usually spurious. The number of human beings endowed with sufficient empathy to penetrate genuinely into another ethnic guise, to take on the world-views, the rules of consciousness of a colored or "third-world" culture, is inevitably very small. Nearly all the Western gurus and publicists who proclaim the new penitential ecumenism, who profess to be brothers under the skin with the roused, vengeful soul of Asia or Africa, are living a rhetorical lie. They are, in the sharpest sense, *en fausse situation.* By virtue of the false loyalties which it commands, this situation is further eroding our emotional, intellectual reserves. If we are to understand where, in political, social terms, the classic past went wrong, we must acknowledge not only the incomparable human creativity of that past but also our enduring, though problematic links with it.

At present, however, such a plea is illusory. The confident center is, I think, unrecapturable. *Rome n'est plus dans Rome.*

Lost also, I would judge—or at least, decisively damaged

—is the axiom of progress, the assumption, dynamic in its self-evidence, that the curve of Western history was ascendant. Doubtless, there were challenges to this presupposition. I have pointed before to a kind of counterclockwise motion of myth, to the widely held intimations, part theological, part romantic-pastoral, of a lapsed paradise and golden age. But even at their most poignant, these Arcadias did not refute a dominant sense of gain. To an astonishing degree, general feeling suppressed even such dramatic monitions of ultimate ruin as were put forward by the study of entropy and heat-death from the 1820s on. The desolate vision of "eternal return," of all history as gyre and *déjà-vu*, as we find it in Nietzsche and in Yeats remained an eccentric nightmare. Common sense held otherwise: although there were bound to be temporary setbacks, agonizing detours, and blind alleys, although the arrow might, at times, seem to fly with enigmatic slowness, history was moving forward. Socially, intellectually, in respect of resources and vistas, civilized man was on the march. Indeed, the steadiness of his tread distinguished him from the inertia, from the myth-enclosed stasis of the "savage." (Only poetry and the fine arts, as Marx noted, seemed to offer a teasing anomaly, having long ago attained a pitch of mastery perhaps unequaled, and surely unsurpassed, since.) So far as the major agencies of history went, progress was not a dogma but a simple matter of observation. In this conviction Hegel and Marx were at one. So also were Darwin and Samuel

Smiles, whose epochal and curiously parallel books, *Origin of Species* and *Self-Help*, appeared in the same month in 1859, at the noon point of a confident era.

Not much of that axiomatic presumption (for it was that) is left to us. The Kierkegaardian concept of "total possibility," of a fabric of reality open at all points to the rift of absurdity and disaster, has become a commonplace. We are back in a politics of torture and of hostages. Public and private violence laps at the foundations of the city, mining, making an acid mark, as does the brown water in Venice. Our threshold of apprehension has been formidably lowered. When the first reports of the death camps were smuggled out of Poland, they were largely disbelieved: such things could not be taking place in civilized Europe, in the mid-twentieth century. Today, it is difficult to conjecture a bestiality, a lunacy of oppression or sudden devastation, which would not be credible, which would not soon be located in the order of facts. Morally, psychologically, it is a terrible thing to be so unastonished. Inevitably, the new realism conspires with what is, or should be, least acceptable in reality.

We do not, moreover, tend to think of the current climate of extremity as a momentary backsliding, as a nasty patch soon to be left behind. This is decisive. Call it *Kulturpessimismus*—it is no accident that the idiom is German—or a new stoic realism. We no longer experience history as ascendant. There are too many cardinal points at which our lives are more threatened, more prone to arbitrary servitude and extermination, than were those of civilized men and women in the West at any time since the late sixteenth century. Soberly, our prognostication must be that of Edgar in *King Lear*:

> And worse I may be yet: the worst is not
> So long as we can say "This is the worst."

Yet, at the same time, our material forward motion is immense and obvious. The "miracles" of technology, medicine, scientific understanding are precisely that. Far more human beings than ever before have a chance of living to maturity, of bearing normal children, of moving upward from the millennial treadmill of marginal subsistence. To overlook a truth so evident and humane is to commit rank snobbery. "Imagine a world without chloroform," urged C. S. Lewis.

But it is also a truth that mocks us. It does so in two ways —both remote from the rationalist meliorism of the Enlightenment and the Victorians. We know now, as Adam Smith and Macaulay did not, that material progress is implicated in a dialectic of concomitant damage, that it destroys irreparable equilibria between society and nature. Technical advances, superb in themselves, are operative in the ruin of primary living systems and ecologies. Our sense of historical motion is no longer linear, but as of a spiral. We can now conceive of a technocratic, hygienic utopia functioning in a void of human possibilities.

The second mock is one of disparity. We no longer ac-

cept the projection, implicit in the classic model of beneficent capitalism, that progress will necessarily spread from
privileged centers to all men. Indecent superfluities in developed societies coexist with what seems to be endemic
starvation over a large part of the earth. In effect, improvement in the chance and duration of individual life, as
brought on by medical technology, has fueled the cycle of
overpopulation and hunger. Often, the supplies and dis-
tributive means required to stop famine and poverty are
available, but inertias of greed or politics stand in the way.
In too many cases the new technocracy is not only destructive
of preceding and alternative values but cruelly impotent
beyond local and profitable appliance. Thus we find ourselves in an ambivalent, ironic stance towards the dogma
of progress and towards the fantastic well-being which so
many of us, in the technological West, actually enjoy.

There are virtues to this ambivalence. Already as argued
in Rousseau and in Godwin, the doctrine of perfectibility
had its muscular complacencies. We cannot separate a sense
of coarse fiber and even of fatuity from much of nineteenth-
century optimism. Our current habituation to nightmare
is not only a safeguard—the tongue sliding over an aching
tooth to domesticate pain—but also an adherence to the
"reality principle." In Freudian terminology, we have come
of age. But at a price. We have lost a characteristic élan, a
metaphysic and technique of "forward dreaming" (of
which Ernst Bloch's *Das Prinzip Hoffnung* is the inspired

statement). No sensibility before ours would, I think, have joined the adjective "dirty" to the word "hope" as did Anouilh in that bleak phrase in *Antigone*: "le sale espoir."

The damage is hard to assess. At vital points our disenchantment is a betrayal of the past. It may well be that the messianic program of social liberation was blind from the start, that Marx's vision of "an altered new basis of production emerging from the historical process" was not only naïve but had in it the germ of future tyranny. It may be that the felt image of the sciences as servants and liberators of society and the spirit—an image so vivid in Wordsworth, in Auguste Comte—was thoughtless from the outset and certain to breed illusion. But the nobility of these errors is unquestionable, as was their energizing function. Much of the truest of our culture was animate with ontological utopia. It is modesty and realism to put aside the millenarian dream, but mendacious to deny the luck of those who dreamt it. Or to forget that our new clear-sightedness stems directly from a catastrophic failure of human possibility.

It is not certain, moreover, than one can devise a model of culture, a heuristic program for further advance, without a utopian core. The question "towards what end effort, towards what end the labor," regresses quickly either towards an obscure instinctual scheme or towards an a priori of hope anchored less in phenomenology, in the actual lines of history, than it is in a dream of ascent:

Dans l'ombre immense du Caucase,
Depuis des siècles, en rêvant,
Conduit par les hommes d'extase,
Le genre humain marche en avant;
Il marche sur la terre; il passe,
Il va dans la nuit, dans l'espace,
Dans l'infini, dans le borné,
Dans l'azur, dans l'onde irritée,
A la lueur de Prométhée,
Le libérateur enchainé!*

All the spent counters of energizing vision are there: the ecstatic leaders, the forward march of humanity as in a dream, the Promethean symbol of life-giving rebellion, instrumental to Marx as it had been to Shelley. How are we, who no longer share Victor Hugo's confidence, for whom history is not, or only diffusely and ironically, a *marche en avant*, to find other reinsurance? A pessimistic critique of culture is a positive construct. And even satire, and there lies its formal strength, worked from or against an implicit postulate of utopia. We no longer avail ourselves of that "compensating heaven" which gave to the static or circular sociologies of medieval and pre-Renaissance thought their dynamic, aspiring imbalance. How is

*In the immense shadow of the Caucasus, / Since centuries, as in a dream, / Led by ecstatic men, / The human race marches ahead. / It marches over the earth; it passes on, / It moves forward in the night, through space, / Through boundless and through enclosed regions, / In the azure of the skies, across the roused seas. / Mankind moves forward by the light of Prometheus, / The chained liberator!

a linear model, with an explicit vector of forward gain, such as aligned and magnetized our sensibilities since at least the seventeenth century, to be underwritten? Nothing *except reality* has schooled us for stasis or regress.

This whole issue of a working theory of culture in the absence of a dogma or genuinely felt metaphoric imperative of progress and perfectibility seems to me one of the most difficult now facing us. The key diagnostic insight is that of Dante when he analyzes the exact condition of prophecy in Hell:

> Però comprender puoi che tutta morta
> fia nostra conoscenza da quel punto,
> che del futuro fia chiusa la porta.*
>
> [*Inferno* 10]

"Close the door of the future"—that is, relinquish the ontological axiom of historical progress—and "all knowledge" is made inert.

The third axiom which we can no longer put forward without extreme qualification is that which correlates humanism—as an educational program, as an ideal referent—to humane social conduct. The issue needs careful statement. The ideology of liberal education, of a classically based humanism in the nineteenth-century scheme of culture, is a working out of specific expectations of the Enlightment. It takes place on many levels, among them

---

You may understand, therefore, / That all our knowledge shall be a dead thing from that moment on / When the door of the future is shut.

university reform, revisions of the school syllabus, expansion of the educational base, adult instruction, the dissemination of excellence through low-cost books and periodicals. These expectations, Lockeian, Jeffersonian if you will, had grown diffuse and self-evident, or self-evident because diffuse (universality entailing vagueness). But their central tenet was clear: that there was a natural progression from the cultivation of feeling and intellect in the individual to rational, beneficent behavior in and by the relevant society. The secular dogma of moral and political progress through education was precisely that: a transfer into the categories of schooling and public enlightenment—the lyceum, the public library, the workingmen's college—of those dynamics of illumination, of human growth towards ethical perfection that had once been theological and transcendentally elective. Thus the Jacobin slogan that the schoolroom was the temple and moral forum of a free people marks the secularization of a utopian, ultimately religious contract between the actuality and the potential of man.

Human folly and cruelty were directly expressive of ignorance, of that injustice whereby the great inheritance of philosophic, artistic, scientific achievements had been transmitted only to a privileged caste. For both Voltaire and Matthew Arnold—and between them they may be said to date and define the generations of cultural promise—there is an obvious congruence between the cultivation of the individual mind through formal knowledge and a melioration in the commanding qualities of life. Though they argued in different idioms and brought different elements to their syllogism, Voltaire and Arnold regarded as established the crucial lemma that the humanities humanize. The root of the "humane" is explicit in both terms, and etymology knits them close. All this is familiar ground.

But the proposition needs to be refined. Although concepts of "nurture," of "culture," and of social melioration or perfectibility were intimately meshed and, often, interchangeable, the precise fabric of the relations between them, of the instrumentalities that led from one to the other, continued to be examined. We do find a good deal of boisterous confidence in the immediate correlation of better schooling with an improved society—particularly in American progressive doctrines and Victorian socialism. But we find also, at a higher plane of debate, a continual awareness of the complexity of the equation. The *Essays on a Liberal Education*, edited by F. W. Farrar in 1867, two years before Arnold's *Culture and Anarchy* and three years before the Education Act, are a representative example of how the general axiom of improvement through humanism was revalued, as it were, from within. What concerned Farrar, Henry Sidgwick, and their colleagues was, precisely, the limitations of the classical canon. They were engaged in reexamining the orthodox notion of a classical literacy, and they were testing its appropriateness to the needs of an increasingly technological and socially diversified community.

In the most incisive of these essays Sidgwick argues for
the extension of the concept of necessary culture to include
modern letters and some competence in the sciences. Greek
and Latin literature can no longer be said to comprise all
essential knowledge, even in an idealized, paradigmatic
form: the claim of these literatures "to give the best teaching in mental, ethical, and political philosophy" is rapidly
passing away. Physical science "is now so bound up with
all the interests of mankind" that some familiarity with it
is indispensable to an understanding of and participation
in "the present phase of the progress of humanity." In
short, the techniques and substantive content of cultural
transmission were under vigorous debate even at the height
of nineteenth-century optimism. What was *not* under
debate was the compelling inference that such transmission,
if and wherever rightly carried out, would lead necessarily
to a more stable, humanely responsible condition of man.
"A liberal education," wrote Sidgwick, with every implication of stating the obvious, "has for its object to impart the
highest culture, to lead youths to the most full, vigorous,
and harmonious exercise, according to the best ideal attain-
able, of their active, cognitive, and aesthetic faculties." Set
in full play, extended, gradually and with due regard to
differing degrees of native capacity, to an ever-widening
compass of society and the globe, such education would
ensure a steadily rising quality of life. Where culture flourished, barbarism was, by definition, a nightmare from the
past.

We know now that this is not so. We know that the formal excellence and numerical extension of education need not correlate with increased social stability and political rationality. The demonstrable virtues of the *Gymnasium* or of the *lycée* are no guarantor of how or whether the city will vote at the next plebiscite. We now realize that extremes of collective hysteria and savagery can coexist with a parallel conservation and, indeed, further development of the institutions, bureaucracies, and professional codes of high culture. In other words, the libraries, museums, theatres, universities, research centers, in and through which the transmission of the humanities and of the sciences mainly takes place, can prosper next to the concentration camps. The discriminations and freshness of their enterprise may well suffer under the surrounding impress of violence and regimentation. But they suffer surprisingly little. Sensibility (particularly that of the performing artist), intelligence, scruple in learning, carry forward as in a neutral zone. We know also—and here is knowledge thoroughly documented but in no way, as yet, incorporated in a rational psychology —that obvious qualities of literate response, of aesthetic feeling, can coexist with barbaric, politically sadistic behavior in the same individual. Men such as Hans Frank who administered the "final solution" in eastern Europe were avid connoisseurs and, in some instances, performers of Bach and Mozart. We know of personnel in the bureaucracy of the torturers and of the ovens who cultivated a knowledge of Goethe, a love of Rilke. The facile evasion; "such men did not understand the poems they read or the music they knew and seemed to play so well," will not do. There simply is no evidence that they were more obtuse than anyone else to the humane genius, to the enacted moral energies of great literature and of art. One of the principal works that we have in the philosophy of language, in the total reading of Hölderlin's poetry, was composed almost within earshot of a death camp. Heidegger's pen did not stop nor his mind go mute.

Whenever I cite this material, I am met with the objection: "Why are you astonished? Why did you expect otherwise? One ought always to have known that culture and humane action, literacy and political impulse, are in no necessary or sufficient correlation." This objection sounds cogent, but it is in fact inadequate to the enormity of the case. The insights we now have into the negative or, at the least, dialectically paradoxical and parodistic relations between culture and society are something new, and morally bewildering. They would have impressed the Enlightenment and much of the nineteenth century as a morbid fantasy (it is precisely Kierkegaard's and Nietzsche's premonitions on this issue that set them apart). Our present knowledge of a negative transfer from civilization to behavior, in the individual and the society, runs counter to the faith, to the operative assumptions, on which the progress of education, of general literacy, of scholarship and the dissemination of the arts were grounded. What we now know makes a mock of the vision of history penetrated, made malleable by, intelligence and educated feeling—a vision common to Jefferson and to Marx, as it was to Arnold and the reformers of 1867. To say that one "ought" to have known is a facile use of language. *Had* the Enlightenment and the nineteenth century understood that there could be no presumption of a carry-over from civilization to civility, from humanism to the humane, the springs of hope would have been staunched and much of the immense liberation of the mind and of society achieved over four generations been rendered impossible. No doubt, confidence should have been less. Perhaps the trust in culture was itself hubristic and blind to the countercurrents and nostalgias for destruction it carried within. It may be that the incapacity of reason and of political will to impede the massacres of 1915-17 ought to have proved a final warning as to the fragility and mutually isolated condition of the fabric of culture.

But our insights here (and they are strangely absent from Eliot's own *Notes* of 1948) come after the facts. They are themselves—this is the main point—a part of desolation. No less than our technical competence to build Hell on earth, so our knowledge of the failure of education, of literate tradition, to bring "sweetness and light" to men, is a clear symptom of what is lost. We are forced now to return to an earlier, Pascalian pessimism, to a model of history whose logic derives from a postulate of original sin. We can subscribe today, all too readily, to de Maistre's view that the barbarism of modern politics, the regress of educated, technologically inventive man into slaughter en-act a necessary working out of the eschatology of the Fall. But there is in our reversion to these earlier, more "realistic" paradigms an element which is spurious and therefore psychologically corrosive. Unlike Pascal or de Maistre, very few of us in fact hold a dogmatic, explicitly religious view of man's personal and social disasters. For most of us the logic of original trespass and the image of history as purgatorial are, at best, a metaphor. Our pessimistic vision, unlike that of a true Jansenist, has neither a rationale of causality nor a hope in transcendent remission. We are caught in the middle. We cannot echo Carducci's famous salute to the future:

> Salute, o genti umane affaticate!
> Tutto trapassa, e nullo può morir.
> Noi troppo odiammo e sofferimo. Amate:
> Il mondo è bello e santo è l'avvenir.*

But we cannot respond either, with full, honest acquiescence, to the Pascalian diagnosis of the cruelties and absurdities of the historical condition as a natural consequence of a primal theological fault.

This instability of essential terrain and the psychological evasions which it entails, characterize much of our current posture. At once realistic and psychologically hollow, our new stoic or ironic pessimism is a determinant of a post-

*Hail to you, oh wearied races of men! / Everything passes, and nothing can die. / We have hated and borne too much. Love one another: / The world is beauteous and the future is holy.

culture. Not to have known about the inhuman potentialities of cultured man what we now know was a formidable privilege. In the generations from Voltaire to Arnold,
absence of such knowledge was not innocence but rather
an enabling program for civilization.

We may be able to group these "irreparables" under an
inclusive heading. The loss of a geographic-sociological
centrality, the abandonment or extreme qualification of the
axiom of historical progress, our sense of the failure or
severe inadequacies of knowledge and humanism in regard
to social action—all these signify the end of an agreed
hierarchic value-structure. Those binary cuts which organized social perception and which represented the domina-
tion of the cultural over the natural code are now blurred or
rejected outright. Cuts between Western civilization and
the rest, between the learned and the untutored, between
the upper and the lower strata of society, between the authority of age and the dependence of youth, between the
sexes. These cuts were not only diacritical—defining the
identity of the two units in relation to themselves and to
each other—they were expressly horizontal. The line of
division separated the higher from the lower, the greater
from the lesser: civilization from retarded primitivism,
learning from ignorance, social privilege from subservi-
ence, seniority from immaturity, men from women. And
each time, "from" stood also for "above." It is the collapse,
more or less complete, more or less conscious, of these
hierarchized, definitional value-gradients (and can there be

value without hierarchy?) which is now the major fact of our intellectual and social circumstance.

The horizontal "cuts" of the classic order have been made vertical and often indistinct.

Never again, I imagine, will a white statesman write as did Palmerston in 1863, at the occasion of a punitive action in far places, "I am inclined to think that our relations with Japan are going through the usual and unavoidable stages of the Intercourse of strong and Civilised nations with weaker and less civilised ones" (even the capitalization speaks loud). A ubiquitous anthropology, relativistic, non-evaluative in its study of differing races and cultures, now pervades our image of "self" and "others." "Countercultures" and aggregates of individualized, ad hoc reference are replacing set discriminations between learning and illiteracy. The line between education and ignorance is no longer self-evidently hierarchic. Much of the mental performance of society now transpires in a middle zone of personal eclecticism. The altering tone and substance of relations between age groups is a commonplace, and one that penetrates almost every aspect of social usage. So, more recently, is the fission of traditional sexual modes. The typologies of women's liberation, of the new politically, socially ostentatious homosexuality (notably in the United States) and of "unisex" point to a deep reordering or disordering of long-established frontiers. "So loosly disally'd," in Milton's telling phrase, men and women are not only maneuvering in a neutral terrain of indistinction, but exchanging roles

—sartorially, psychologically, in regard to economic and erotic functions which were formerly set apart.

Again, a general rubric suggests itself. A common formlessness or search for new forms has all but undermined classic age-lines, sexual divisions, class structures, and hierarchic gradients of mind and power. We are caught in a Brownian movement at every vital, molecular level of individuation and society. And if I may carry the analogy one step further, the membranes through which social energies are current are now permeable and nonselective.

It is widely asserted that the rate of social change we are experiencing is unprecedented, that metamorphoses and hybridizations across lines of time, of sexuality, of race, are now occurring more quickly than ever before. Does this rate and universality of change reflect verifiable organic transformations? This is a very difficult question to pose accurately, let alone to answer. We "undergo" much of reality, sharply filtered and pre-sensed, through the instant diagnostic sociology of the mass media. No previous society has mirrored itself with such profuse fascination. At present, models and mythologies of fact, quite often astute and seemingly comprehensive, are offered at bewildering short intervals. This rapidity and "metadepth" of explanation may be obscuring the distinction between what is a matter of fashion, of surface coloration, and what occurs at the internal levels of a psychological or social system. What we know of the evolutionary time-scale makes it highly improbable that psychophysiological changes are happening in a dramatic, observable rhythm. To take an example: far-reaching correlations are being drawn between a revolution in sexual mores and the presumed lowering in the age of menstruation. It would appear that this phenomenology is susceptible of exact statistical inquiry. But, in fact, material and methodological doubts abound. What cultures or communities are affected, and how many cases within them would constitute a critical mass? Are we dealing with primary or secondary symptoms, with a physiological change or one in the context of awareness and social acceptance? Granted the fact, is the correlation legitimate, or are parallel but essentially dissociated mechanisms at work? Skepticism is in order.

Yet there ought also to be a certain largesse and vulnerability of imagination. It is conceivable, to put it modestly, that current changes in patterns of nutrition, of temperature control, of quick travel across climates and time zones, that the prolongation of the average life-span, and the ingestion of therapeutic and narcotic substances, *are* bringing on genuine modification of personality, and marginally, perhaps, of physique. Such changes could be defined as "intermediary mutations," somewhere between the organic and the modish—in the strong sense of that term. We have no exact vocabulary in which to express second-order psychosocial or sociophysiological metamorphoses. Nevertheless, these seem to me to be the most important variant in the whole of post-culture.

Much of this is common ground. So, also, is the insight,

first expressed by Benda, still the acutest of cultural critics, that the breakdown of classic hierarchies would occur from within. Wherever a decisive breach has been opened in the lines of order, the sappers have tunneled from inside the city. The conscience of privilege, of seniority, of mandarin rights has turned against itself.

Less widely asked is the question of whether certain core-elements in the classic hierarchy of values are even worth reanimating? Is there a conceivable defense of the concept of culture against the two principal attacks now being pressed home? Particularly if we adhere to Eliot's central proposition "that culture is not merely the sum of several activities, but a *way of life*."

It is on the fragility and cost of that "way of life" that the attack has borne. Why labor to elaborate and transmit culture if it did so little to stem the inhuman, if there were in it deep-set ambiguities which, at times, even solicited barbarism? Secondly: granted that culture was a medium of human excellence and intellectual vantage, was the price paid for it too high? In terms of social and spiritual inequality. In regard to the ontological imbalance—it ran deeper than economics—between the privileged locale of intellectual and artistic achievement, and the excluded world of poverty and underdevelopment. Can it have been accident that a large measure of ostentatious civilization—in Periclean Athens, in the Florence of the Medicis, in sixteenth-century England, in the Versailles of the *grand siècle* and the Vienna of Mozart—was closely correlate with political absolutism, a firm caste system, and the surrounding presence of a subject populace? Great art, music, and poetry, the science of Bacon and of Laplace, flourish under more or less totalitarian modes of social governance. Can this be hazard? How vital are the affinities between power relations and classic literacy (relations initiated in the teaching process)? Is not the very notion of culture tautological with élitism? How many of its major energies feed on the violence which is disciplined, contained within, yet ceremonially visible, in a traditional or repressive society? Hence Pisarev's critique, echoed later in Orwell, of art and letters as instrumentalities of caste and régime.

These are the challenges put contemptuously by the dropout and loud in the four-letter graffiti of the "counter-culture." What good did high humanism do the oppressed mass of the community? What use was it when barbarism came? What immortal poem has ever stopped or mitigated political terror—though a number have celebrated it? And, more searchingly: Do those for whom a great poem, a philosophic design, a theorem, are, in the final reckoning, the supreme value, not help the throwers of napalm by looking away, by cultivating in themselves a stance of "objective sadness" or historical relativism?

I have tried to suggest, throughout this essay, that there is no adequate answer to the question of the frailty of culture. We can construe all kinds of post facto insight into the lack of correlation between literarcy and politics, be-

tween the inheritance of Weimar and the reality of Buchen-
wald not many kilometers away. But diagnosis after the
event is, at best, a shallow and partial comprehension. So
far as I can see, much of the harrowing puzzle remains.

The question as to whether a high culture is not inevitably
meshed with social injustice can be answered. It is not difficult to formulate an apologia for civilization based firmly
and without cant on a model of history as privilege, as
hierarchic order. One can say simply that the accomplish-
ments of art, of speculative imagining, of the mathematical
and empirical sciences have been, are, will be, to an overwhelming extent, the creation of the gifted few. In the
perspective of the evolution of the species towards an even
more complete enlistment of the potentialities of the cortex
—and the sum of history may be precisely that—it is vital
to preserve the kind of political system in which high gifts
are recognized and afforded the pressures under which they
flourish. The existence of a Plato, of a Karl Friedrich Gauss,
of a Mozart may go a surprisingly long way towards re-
deeming that of man. The immense majority of human
biographies are a gray transit between domestic spasm and
oblivion. For a truly cultured sensibility to deny this, under
pretexts of liberal piety, is not only mendacious but rank
ingratitude. A culture "lived" is one that draws for con-
tinuous, indispensable sustenance on the great works of
the past, on the truths and beauties achieved in the tradition.
It does not reckon against them the social harshness, the
personal suffering, which so often have generated or made

possible the symphony, the fresco, the metaphysic. Where
it is absolutely honest, the doctrine of a high culture will
hold the burning of a great library, the destruction of Galois
at twenty-one, or the disappearance of an important score,
to be losses paradoxically but none the less decidedly out of
proportion with common deaths, even on a large scale.

This is a coherent position. It may accord with deep-
seated biological realities. For perfectly obvious reasons,
however, it is a position which few today are ready to put
forward publicly or with conviction. It flies too drastically
in the face of doubts about culture which we have seen to
be justified. It is too crassly out of tune with pervasive ideals
of humane respect and social concern. There is something
histrionic and psychologically suspect even in the bare exercise of stating an élitist canon.

But it is important to see just why this is so. Using the
terms I have indicated, and made with complete honesty,
a contemporary defense of culture as "a way of life" will
nevertheless have a void at its center. To argue for order
and classic values on a purely immanent, secular basis is,
finally, implausible. In stressing this point Eliot is justified,
and the *Notes towards the Definition of Culture* remain
valid. But if the core of a theory of culture is "religious,"
that term ought not to be taken, as it so largely was by
Eliot, in a particular sectarian sense. If only because of its
highly ambiguous implication in the holocaust, Christianity
cannot serve as the focus of a redefinition of culture, and
Eliot's nostalgia for Christian discipline is now the most

vulnerable aspect of his argument. I mean "religious" in a particular and more ancient sense. What is central to a true culture is a certain view of the relations between time and individual death.

The thrust of will which engenders art and disinterested thought, the engaged response which alone can ensure its transmission to other human beings, to the future, are rooted in a gamble on transcendence. The writer or thinker means the words of the poem, the sinews of the argument, the personae of the drama, to outlast his own life, to take on the mystery of autonomous presence and presentness. The sculptor commits to the stone the vitalities against and across time which will soon drain from his own living hand. Art and mind address those who are not yet, even at the risk, deliberately incurred, of being unnoticed by the living.

There is nothing natural, nothing self-evident in this wager against mortality, against the common, unharried promises of life. In the overwhelming majority of cases— and the gambler on transcendence knows this in advance— the attempt will be a failure, nothing will survive. There may be a cancerous mania in the mere notion of producing great art or philosophic shapes—acts, by definition, free of utility and immediate reward. Flaubert howled like a man racked at the thought that Emma Bovary—his creature, his contrivance of arrayed syllables—would be alive and real, long after he himself had gone to a painful death. There is a calm enormity, the more incisive for its deliberate scriptural echo, in Pope's assertion that "to follow Poetry as one ought, one must forget father and mother, and cleave to it alone." For "Poetry" in that sentence, one can read mathematics, music, painting, astrophysics, or whatever else consumes the spirit with total demand.

Each time, the equation is one of ambitious sacrifice, of the obsession to outlast, to outmaneuver the banal democracy of death. To die at thirty-five but to have composed *Don Giovanni*, to know, as did Galois during the last night of his twenty-one-year existence, that the pages he was writing would alter the future forms of algebra and of space. Perhaps an insane conceit, using that term in its stylistic sense, but one that is the transcendent source of a classic culture.

We hear it proclaimed at the close of Pindar's Third Pythian Ode (in Lattimore's version):

> I will work out the divinity that is busy within my mind
> and tend the means that are mine.
> Might God only give me luxury and its power,
> I hope I should find glory that would rise higher hereafter.
> Nestor and Sarpedon of Lykia we know,
> men's speech, from the sounding words that smiths of
>   song in their wisdom
> built to beauty. In the glory of poetry achievement of men
> blossoms long; but of that the accomplishment is given to
>   few.

Note the modulation from poetic action to aristocratic truth

—"but of that the accomplishment is given to few." It is not accidental. The trope of immortality persists in Western culture, is central to it, from Pindar to the time of Mallarmé's vision of *le Livre*, "tenté à son insu par quiconque a écrit," which is the very aim of the universe. The obsession is crystallized once more, memorably, in Eluard's phrase "le dur désir de durer." Without such "harsh longing" there may be human love and justice, mercy and scruple. But can there be a true culture? Can civilization as we know it be underwritten by an immanent view of personal and social reality? Can it be vital without a logic of relation between "the divinity that is busy within my mind" and the hunger for a "glory that would rise higher hereafter"? And it is precisely that logic, with its inference of active afterlife in and through artistic, intellectual creation, which is "religious."

This logic and its idiom are now eroded. The notion, axiomatic in classic art and thought, of sacrificing present life, present humanity, to the marginal chance of future literary or intellectual renown, grates on modern nerves. To younger people today, the code of "glory" of intellect and creative act is highly suspect. Many would see in it no more than romantic bathos or a disguised perpetuation of élitist idols. There are currently, particularly in the United States, some fashionable, silly theories about total revolutions of consciousness. Mutations of internal structure do not occur at such rate. But in this key matter of the equivocations between *poiesis*—the artist's, the thinker's creation

—and death, deep shifts of perspective *are* discernible. Psychologically, there is a gap of light years between the sensibility of my own schooling, in the French formal vein, with its obvious stress on the prestige of genius and the compulsion of creative survival, and the posture of my students today. Do they still name city squares after algebraists?

The causes of this change are multiple. They may involve elements as different as the standardization of death in two world wars and the "bomb culture," and the emergence of a new collectivism. An analysis of these currents lies outside the scope of this essay, but the symptoms are plain to see. They include the ideology of the "happening" and of autodestructive artifacts, with their emphasis on the immediacy, unrepeatability, and ephemeral medium of the work. Aleatory music is a striking case of the diminution of creative authority in favor of collaborative, spontaneous shadow-play (Werner Henze has declared that there is exploitation and the menace of arbitrary power in the very function of the composer). More and more literary texts and works of art now offer themselves as collective and/or anonymous. The poetics of ecstasy and of group feeling regard the imprint of a single "great name" on the process of creation as archaic vanity. The audience is no longer an informed echo to the artist's talent, a respondent to and transmitter of his singular enterprise; it is joint creator in a conglomerate of freewheeling, participatory impulse. Away with the presumptions of permanence in a classic *œuvre*, away with masters.

It would be absurd to try and pass judgment on the merits of this new "leveling"—I use the word because there are obscure but substantive precedents in seventeenth-century Adamic and millenary dreams of all men as artists and equal singers of the moment. I am only saying that if this revaluation of the criteria of "lastingness," of individual mastery against time, is as radical and far-reaching as it now seems, the core of the very concept of culture will have been broken. If the gamble on transcendence no longer seems worth the odds and we are moving into a utopia of the immediate, the value-structure of our civilization will alter, after at least three millennia, in ways almost unforseeable.

Speaking with the serene malice of age and work done, Robert Graves has recently asserted that "Nothing can stop the wide destruction of our ancient glories, amenities and pleasures." This may be too large a sweep, and in place of "destruction" it might be better to say "transmutation," "change." Nevertheless, it is almost certain that the old vocabulary is exhausted, that the forms of classic culture cannot be rebuilt on any general scale.

4 · Tomorrow

WWould that I were able to bring this argument to a resonant close, that I might end on a rounded note of promise. "It is no longer possible," remarked Eliot, "to find consolation in prophetic gloom." The "pressing needs of an emergency," to which he referred twenty years ago, have become more drastic since. We feel ourselves tangled in a constant, lashing web of crisis.

Whether this feeling is entirely legitimate remains a fair question. There have been previous stages of extreme pressure on and within Western civilization. It is only now, in the provisional light of currently fashionable "archaeologies of consciousness," that we are beginning to gauge what must have been the climate of nerve during the known approach and blaze of pestilence in late medieval and seventeenth-century Europe. What, one wonders, were the mechanics of hope, indeed of the future tense itself, during the Hunnish invasions? Read Michelet's narrative of life in Paris in 1420. Who, in the closing phases of the Thirty Years' War, when, as chroniclers put it, there were only wolves for wolves to feed on in the empty towns, foresaw the near upsurge of cultural energies and the counterbalancing strength of the Americas? It may be that our frame work of apocalypse, even where it is low-keyed and ironic, is dangerously inflationary. Perhaps we exaggerate both the rate and vehemence of crisis—in international affairs, where there has, on the large scale, been a quarter century of peace under unlikely conditions; in the ecology, which has been savaged before (witness the man-made Sahara) and has recovered; in society and personal consciousness, both of which have known previous moments of extreme challenge. A thread of hysteria runs through our current "realism." One can imagine Pangloss putting forward a reasoned plea for the humaneness and felicity of the times. But, adds Voltaire, "ayant soutenu une fois que tout allait à merveille, il le soutenait toujours, et n'en croyait rien." Nor do we. Whether or not our intimations of utter menace are justified is not the issue. They permeate our sensibility. It is inside them that the post-culture conducts its fragmented, often contradictory business.

At best, therefore, I can offer conjectures as to what may be synapses worth watching. The picture is one of unparalleled complication and rate of change (the life of Churchill covered the span from a battle fought at Omdurman on horseback with swords, in a manner almost Homeric, to the construction of the hydrogen bomb). I can, perhaps, make some guesses, not with a view to prophetic aptness, but in the hope that they might be erroneous in a way that will retain a documentary interest. I shall focus on the question of a new literacy, of that minimal gamut of shared recognitions and designative codes without which there can be neither a coherent society nor a continuation, however attenuated, however transitional, of a "lived culture." Even in this limited purpose, one is made conscious of Blake's exasperation at "the idiot questioner." The asking, today, is so much more incisive, so much more flattering to one's intelligence, than the blurred reply.

We have seen something of the collapse of hierarchies and of the radical changes in the value-systems which relate personal creation with death. These mutations have brought an end to classic literacy. By that I mean something perfectly concrete. The major part of Western literature, which has been for two thousand years and more so deliberately interactive, the work echoing, mirroring, alluding to previous works in the tradition, is now passing quickly out of reach. Like far galaxies bending over the horizon of invisibility, the bulk of English poetry, from Caxton's Ovid to *Sweeney among the Nightingales*, is now modulating from active presence into the inertness of scholarly conservation. Based, as it firmly is, on a deep, many-branched anatomy of classical and scriptural reference, expressed in a syntax and vocabulary of heightened tenor, the unbroken arc of English poetry, of reciprocal discourse that relates Chaucer and Spenser to Tennyson and to Eliot, is fading rapidly from the reach of natural reading. A central pulse in awareness, in the language, is becoming archival. Though complex in its causes and consequences, this dimming of recognitions is easy to demonstrate:

> Yet once more, O ye laurels, and once more,
> Ye myrtles brown, with ivy never sere,
> I come to pluck your berries harsh and crude,
> And with forced fingers rude
> Shatter your leaves before the mellowing year.
> Bitter constraint, and sad occasion dear,
> Compels me to disturb your season due;

> For Lycidas is dead, dead ere his prime,
> Young Lycidas, and hath not left his peer.
> Who would not sing for Lycidas? he knew
> Himself to sing, and build the lofty rhyme.

Laurel, myrtle, and ivy have their specific emblematic life throughout Western art and poetry, and within Milton's own work. We read, in his fine tribute to Giovanni Manso:

> Forsitan et nostros ducat de marmore vultus,
> Nectens aut Paphiâ myrti aut Parnasside lauri
> Fronde comas. . . .*

The ivy stands for poetry when it is particularly allied to learning: Horace's *Odes* I. I. 29 and Spenser's *Shepheards Calendar* for September tell us that, as they told it to Milton. *Odes* I is at work also in "myrtles brown" (*pulla myrtus*). The *Shepheards Calendar* for January and *Macbeth*, obviously, are resonant in the use of "sere." And the echo moves forward to Tennyson's *Ode to Memory* and "Those peerless flowers which in the rudest wind / Never grow sere" (*rude* has carried over into Tennyson's ear from Milton's next line). "Hard constraint" has moved Spenser to write his *Pastoral Eclogue* on Sidney, and the entire trope of compulsion is summarized in Keats's *Ode to Psyche*:

> O Goddess! hear these tuneless numbers, wrung
>   By sweet enforcement and remembrance dear.

Perhaps he would produce our features / With Paphian myrtle or Parnassian laurel / Twining our hair. . . .

The Spenser and the Keats phrasings both temper and heighten the special coil of Milton's word order: *sad occasion dear*, in which "dear" signifies whatever affects us most directly, be it in love or in hatred, in pleasure or in grief (cf. *Hamlet*, " my dearest foe in heaven," or *Henry V*, "all your dear offences"). Lycidas is, of course, the name of the shepherd in Theocritus's seventh *Idyl* and that of one of the speakers in the ninth *Eclogue* of Vergil. The immediate reiteration of the name, particularly at the start of the line, is a long-established convention of pathos, a musical augment of sorrow. Spenser's *Astrophel* was probably in Milton's mind:

> Young Astrophel, the pride of shepheards praise,
> Young Astrophel, the rusticke lasses love.

Both "repeats," the Spenserian and the Miltonic, will sound in Shelley's *Adonais*. "Who would not sing for Lycidas?" is almost translation: from Vergil's tenth *Eclogue* 2. 3— "Carmine sunt dicenda; neget quis carmina Gallo"? Cf. the *reprise* in Pope's *Windsor Forest*:

> Granville commands; your aid, O Muses, bring!
> What Muse for Granville can refuse to sing?

And so on.

All these are surface markings. We find them in dictionaries and concordances. They can be put at the bottom of the page in what might be called "first-level footnotes."

But the information they provide is only the outward of literacy.

Fullness of response depends on an accord, almost intuitive because so thoroughly schooled, with the whole nature of Milton's enterprise, with the context of intent, and agreed emotional, designative reflexes on which the poem is built. A natural reading implies an apprehension, generalized but exact, of what is meant by *Idyl* and *Eclogue*, and of the millennial interplay, at once symbolic and conventional, between images of Arcadia and of death. It is an apprehension which includes, for supporting or contrastive reference, not only something of Greek pastoral and a reasonable amount of Vergil, but Giorgione and Poussin. Milton's *monody*, itself a term charged with precise intimations of range and tone, is nearly impossible to get into right focus if one has no acquaintance with that mode of Italian elegiac pastoral, often composed in Latin, in which the world of Arcadia comprises problematic, philosophically resistant elements of contemporary politics and religion. Is any naturalness of response to the text plausible without familiarity, again unobtrusive because long-established, with the grid of seasonal, botanical, and celestial markers that direct the motion of the argument and allow its vital economy (the amaranth, the daystar, the agricultural and liturgical overtones of May)?

To "read" *Lycidas*, to seize its purpose at any level but that of vague musicality, is to participate, and not only with one's brain, in the central equivocation between death and poetic glory. Milton's is one of the archetypal statements of the trope of transcendence, of that cast for immortality beyond "the parching wind." This is a poem about fame and the sacrificial gamble which "scorns delights and lives laborious days." The pulse of allusion that beats steady in almost every line, back to Greek, to Latin, to Scripture, and which echoes forward to Dryden, to Arnold, to Tennyson's *In Memoriam*, is no technical ornament. It is a full-scale pronouncement of accord with the value-relations of personal genius and menacing time which underlie a classic culture. The lament for the poet gone is always autobiographical: the mourner tenses his own resources against the ubiquitous blackmail of death. The "sincerity" of his grief is intense but reflexive. Dissent from this code of moral, psychological conduct, be deaf to its particular idiom, and you will no longer be able to read, to hear, the great tradition of elegy and poetics, of mediation between language and death, which led unbroken from Pindar and Vergil to *Thyrsis* and to Auden's commemoration of the death of William Butler Yeats.

Here, too, there could be footnotes. Conceivably, such "second-level" annotation could refer the reader of *Lycidas* to all the requisite classical, scriptural, and contemporary material. It could tell him of the history of elegiac modes and of Milton's notion, old as Hesiod, of the civilizing and sacramental functions of the shepherd-singer. In fact, of course, such annotation would soon run to incommensurable absurdity (it is this which distinguishes it, though not

always sharply, from what I called "first-level footnotes").
To be genuinely informative, contextual annotation would
soon amount to little less than a history of the language and
of culture. We would find ourselves involved in a process—
familiar to information theory—of infinite regress. The
total context of a work such as *Lycidas*—or the *Divina Commedia* or *Phèdre* or Goethe's *Faust*—is "all that is the case,"
or the active wholeness of preceding and sequent literacy.
The thing cannot be done.

But suppose that it could. Suppose that some masterly
editorial team devised a complete apparatus of explanation,
by virtue of glossaries, concordances, biographical and stylistic appendixes. What will have happened to the poem?

This is the decisive point.

As the glossaries lengthen, as the footnotes become more
elementary and didactic, the poem, the epic, the drama,
moves out of balance on the actual page. As even the more
rudimentary of mythological, religious, or historical references, which form the grammar of Western literature, have
to be elucidated, the lines of Spenser, of Pope, of Shelley,
or of *Sweeney among the Nightingales* blur away from
immediacy. Where it is necessary to annotate every proper
name and classical allusion in the dialogue between Lorenzo
and Jessica in the garden at Belmont, or in Iachimo's
stealthy rhetoric when he emerges in Imogen's chamber,
these marvelous spontaneities of enacted feeling become
"literary" and twice-removed (in part, of course, the problem is one of time, of the mere fact that meaning is no

longer grasped as quickly, as directly, as it is articulated). How is Pope's *Essay on Man* to register its delicate precision and sinew when each proposition reaches us, as it were, on stilts, at the top of a page crowded with elementary comment? What presence in personal delight can *Endymion* have when recent editions annotate "Venus" as signifying "pagan goddess of love"?

These are no rhetorical, futuristic questions. The situation is already on us. In the United States there have appeared versions of parts of the Bible and of Shakespeare in basic English and in strip-cartoon format. Some of these have circulated in the millions. The challenge they represent is serious and credible. It will not be brushed off. We are being asked to choose. Would we have something, at least, of the main legacy of our civilization made accessible to the general public of a modern, mass society? Or would we rather see the bulk of our literature, of our interior history, pass into the museum? The question cannot be evaded by consoling references to paperback sales or to presentations of classic material—excellent as such presentations sometimes are—on the mass media. These are only surface noises and salutations to a past whose splendor and authority are still atavistically recognized.

The issues are compelling and demand the most honest possible response. Already a dominant proportion of poetry, of religious thought, of art, has receded from personal immediacy into the keeping of the specialist. There it leads a kind of bizarre pseudo-life, proliferating its own inert environment of criticism (we read Eliot *on* Dante, not Dante), of editorial and textual exegesis, of narcissistic polemic. Never has there been a more hectic prodigality of specialized erudition—in literary studies, in musicology, in art history, in criticism, and in that most Byzantine of genres, the criticism and theory of criticism. Never have the metalanguages of the custodians flourished more, or with more arrogant jargon, around the silence of live meaning.

An archival pseudovitality surrounding what was once felt life; a semiliteracy or subliteracy outside, making it impossible for the poem to survive naked, to achieve unattended personal impact. Academy and populism. The two conditions are reciprocal, and each polarizes the other in a necessary dialectic. Between them they determine our current state.

The challenge is: Was it ever different?

The answer is not as straightforward as current abrasiveness would suggest. Despite pioneering studies, particularly with regard to the nineteenth century in England, our knowledge of the history of reading habits, of the statistics and quality of literate response at different moments and in different communities of Western Europe, is still rudimentary. Such well-attested but local facts as the wide dissemination and collective study of Godwin's *Political Justice* during the 1790s, or what we know of the sales and circulation of such writers as George Sand and Tennyson, may or may not be more generally indicative. The evidence is hard to come by and harder to assess. One deals with impressionistic notions of "climate" and "tonality."

Nevertheless, certain contours do emerge. Scriptural and, in a wider sense, religious literacy ran strong, particularly in Protestant lands. The Authorized Version and Luther's Bible carried in their wake a rich tradition of symbolic, allusive, and syntactic awareness. Absorbed in childhood, the Book of Common Prayer, the Lutheran hymnal and psalmody cannot but have marked a broad compass of mental life with their exact, stylized articulateness and music of thought. Habits of communication and schooling, moreover, sprang directly from the concentration of memory. So much was learned and known *by heart*—a term beautifully apposite to the organic, inward presentness of meaning and spoken being within the individual spirit. The catastrophic decline of memorization in our own modern education and adult resources is one of the crucial, though as yet little understood, symptoms of an after-culture.

As to knowledge of the classics, here again the evidence varies and is susceptible of different interpretations. But exposure to the forms and conventions active in *Lycidas* was certainly part of a sound education from the seventeenth century until very recently. Different curricula and different social settings obviously entailed varying degrees of depth: but the Homeric and Vergilian epic, the poetry of Ovid and of Horace, the theory of genres in Aristotle and Longinus were no recondite topics. With a few exceptions (mainly those bearing on the Italian and Renaissance-Latin corpus), none of Milton's imitations and pointers would have been outside the scope of my father's schooling in a Vienna *Gymnasium* before the first World War, or indeed outside my own in the *section lettres* of the French *lycée* system of the 1930s and 40s.

The organized amnesia of present primary and secondary education is a very recent development. There is irony in the fact that one associates the main impetus of this change, its frankest theoretic justifications, with the United States. For it was in the North America of the late eighteenth and nineteenth centuries that the ideal, both Puritan and Jeffersonian, of a general biblical and classical literacy was most widely aimed at.

Concentric to these spheres of "book-knowledge" lies a personal, unforced intimacy with the names and shapes of the natural world, with flower and tree, with the measure of the seasons and the rising and setting of the stars. The principal energies of our literature draw constantly on this set of recognitions. But to our housed, metallic sensibilities they have become largely artificial and decorative. Do not, today, inquire of the reader next to you whether he can identify, from personal encounter, even a part of the flora, of the astronomy, which served Ovid and Shakespeare, Spenser and Goethe, as a current alphabet.

Any generalization in these matters is suspect. But the fundamental "polysemic" texture of poetry, drama, and fiction, certainly since the seventeenth century, the writer's deployment of meaning at many simultaneous levels of directness or difficulty, does imply the availability, perhaps utopian, yet perhaps realistic also, of a wide literate public. Heremeticism, the strategy of the incomprehensible, as we find it in so much of art and literature after Mallarmé, is a reaction, haughty and desolate, to the decay of a natural literacy:

> We were the last romantics—chose for theme
> Traditional sanctity and loveliness;
> Whatever's written in what poets name
> The book of the people; whatever most can bless
> The mind of man or elevate a rhyme;
> But all is changed, that high horse riderless,
> Though mounted in that saddle Homer rode
> Where the swan drifts upon a darkening flood.

But let us assume that Yeats's picture is idealized, that Pegasus has gone more often than not bareback. Let us suppose that the Victorian public-school boy, the *Gymnasiast* or *lycéen* to whom the text of Homer, of Racine, of Goethe, offered natural purchase, were always but a small number, a conscious élite. Even if this was so, the case stands. Restricted as it may have been, that élite embodied the inheritance and dynamics of culture. Its social, economic predominance and confident self-perpetuation were such that the model of a culture—whose values may, indeed, have been specialized and minority-based—served as general criterion. This is the point. Power relations, first courtly and aristocratic, then bourgeois and bureaucratic, under-wrote the syllabus of classic culture and made of its transmission a deliberate proceeding. The democratization of high culture—brought on by a crisis of nerve within culture itself and by social revolution—has engendered an absurd hybrid. Dumped on the mass market, the products of classic literacy will be thinned and adulterated. At the opposite end of the spectrum, these same products are salvaged out of life and put in the museum vault.

Again, America is the representative and premonitory example. Nowhere has the debilitation of genuine literacy gone further (consider recent surveys of reading comprehension and recognition in American high schools). But nowhere, also, have the conservation and learned scrutiny of the art or literature of the past been pursued with more generous authority. American libraries, universities, archives, museums, centers for advanced study are now the indispensable record and treasure house of civilization. It is here that the European artist and scholar must come to see the cherished afterglow of his culture. Though often obsessed with the future, the United States is now, certainly in regard to the humanities, the active watchman of the classic past.

It may be that this custodianship relates to a deeply puzzling fact. Creation of absolutely the first rank—in philosophy, in music, in much of literature, in mathematics—continues to occur outside the American milieu. It is at once taken up and intelligently exploited there, but the

"motion of spirit" has taken place elsewhere, amid the en-
ervation of Europe, in the oppressive climate of Russia.
There is, in a good deal of American intellectual, artistic
production (recent painting may be the challenging ex-
ception) a characteristic near-greatness, a strength just below the best. Could it be that the United States is destined
to be the "museum culture"? There is no more fascinating
question in the sociology of knowledge, none that may touch
more intensely on our future. But it lies outside the scope of
this essay.

These changes from a dominant to a post- or subliteracy
are themselves expressed in a general "retreat from the
word." Seen from some future historical perspective, Western civilization, from its Hebraic-Greek origins roughly to
the present, may look like a phase of concentrated "verbal-
ism." What seem to us salient distinctions may appear to
have been parts of a general era in which spoken, remem-
bered, and written discourse was the backbone of consciousness. It is a commonplace of current sociology and "media-
study" that this primacy of the "logic"—of that which
organizes the articulations of time and of meaning around
the *logos*—is now drawing to a close. Increasingly, the
word is caption to the picture. Expanding areas of fact and
of sensibility, notably in the exact sciences and the non-
representational arts, are out of reach of verbal account or
paraphrase. The notations of symbolic logic, the languages
of mathematics, the idiom of the computer, are no longer

metadialects, responsible and reducible to the grammars of verbal cognition. They are autonomous communicatory modes, claiming and expressing for themselves an increasing reach of contemplative and active pursuit. Words are corroded by the false hopes and lies they have voiced. The electronic alphabet of immediate global communication and "togetherness" is not the ancient, divisive legacy of Babel, but the image-in-motion.

Many aspects of this analysis (which was, in fact, put forward some years before McLuhan gave it explosive currency) may well be mistaken or exaggerated. Transmutations of this order of magnitude do not occur overnight and at the immediately graphic surface. But the general "feel" of the argument is persuasive. There *is* a comprehensive decline in traditional ideals of literate speech. Rhetoric and the arts of conviction which it disciplines are in almost total disrepute. Pleasure in style, in the "wroughtness" of expressive forms, is a mandarin, nearly suspect posture. More and more of the informational energy required by a mass-consumer society is being transmitted pictorially. The proportions of articulate charge between margin and column of print is being reversed. We are moving back to a layout of the "spaces of meaning" in which the pictorial bordure preempts more and more of the whole. Often now, it is the shred of text which 'illustrates" (here also, the premonitory presence is that of Blake).

If my previous suggestions are at all valid, it will be obvious where the principal connections lie.

The classic speech-construct, the centrality of the word are informed by and expressive of both a hierarchic value-system and the trope of transcendence. These nodes of sensibility are interactive and mutually reinforcing at every point. Indo-European syntax is an active mirroring of systems of order, of hierarchic dependence, of active and passive stance, such as have been prominent in the fabric of Western society. The cliché tag regarding the capacity of Latin grammar to reproduce characteristic attitudes in Roman feeling and conduct is true in a more acute and general sense. An explicit grammar is an acceptance of order: it is a hierarchization, the more penetrating for being enforced so early in the individual life-span, of the forces and valuations prevailing in the body politic (the tonalities of "class," "classification," and "classic" are naturally cognate). The sinews of Western speech closely enacted and, in turn, stabilized, carried forward, the power relations of the Western social order. Gender differentiations, temporal cuts, the rules governing prefix and suffix formations, the synapses and anatomy of a grammar—these are the *figura*, at once ostensive and deeply internalized, of the commerce between the sexes, between master and subject, between official history and utopian dream, in the corresponding speech community.

The affinities between the preeminence of the word and the classic gamble on and against death are even more central and complex. The ontological and hermeneutic aspects of the modulations between a language-culture and death, explored, for example, in Heidegger and Paul Ricœur, are too demanding to be touched on here. The point is that the very verb-systems of Indo-European langages are "performative" of those attitudes towards act and survival which animate the classic doctrine of knowledge and of art. What the poet terms "glory" is a direct function of the felt reality of the future tense. The ordered density of remembrance hinges on the prodigal exactitudes of Indo-European preterits. Thus the time-death copula of a classic structure of personal and philosophic values is, in many respects, syntactic, and is inherent to a fabric of life in which language holds a sovereign, almost magically validated role. Diminish that role, subvert that eminence, and you will have begun to demolish the hierarchies and transcedence-values of a classic civilization. Even death can be made mute.

The counterculture is perfectly aware of where to begin the job of demolition. The violent illiteracies of the graffiti, the clenched silence of the adolescent, the nonsense-cries from the stage-happening are resolutely strategic. The insurgent and the freak-out have broken off discourse with a cultural system which they despise as a cruel, antiquated fraud. They will not bandy words with it. Accept, even momentarily, the conventions of literate linguistic exchange, and you are caught in the net of the old values, of the grammars that can condescend or enslave.

Changes of idiom between generations are a normal part of social history. Previously, however, such changes and the verbal provocations of young against old have been variants on an evolutionary continuum. What is occurring now is new: it is an attempt at a total break. The mumble of the dropout, the "fuck-off" of the beatnik, the silence of the teenager in the enemy house of his parents are meant to destroy. Cordelia's asceticism, her refusal of the mendacities of speech, proves murderous. So does that of the autistic child when it stamps on language, pulverizing it to gibberish or maniacal silence. We empty of their humanity those to whom we deny speech. We make them naked and absurd. There is a terrible, literal image in "stone-deafness," in the opaque babble or speechlessness of the "stoned." Break off speech to others and the Medusa turns inward. Hence something of the hurt and despair of the present conflict between generations. Deliberate violence is being done to those primary ties of identity and social cohesion produced by a common language.

But are there no other literacies conceivable, "literacies" not of the letter?

This is being written in a study in a college of one of the great American universities. The walls are throbbing gently to the beat of music coming from one near and several more distant amplifiers. The walls quiver to the ear or to the touch roughly eighteen hours per day, sometimes twenty-four. The beat is literally unending. It matters little whether it is that of pop, folk, or rock. What counts is the all-pervasive pulsation, morning to night and into night, made indiscriminate by the cool burn of electronic timbre. A large segment of mankind, between the ages of thirteen and, say, twenty-five, now lives immersed in this constant throb. The hammering of rock or of pop creates an enveloping space. Activities such as reading, writing, private communication, learning, previously framed with silence, now take place in a field of strident vibrato. This means that the essentially linguistic nature of these pursuits is adulterated; they are vestigial modes of the old "logic."

The new sound-sphere is global. It ripples at great speed across languages, ideologies, frontiers, and races. The triplet pounding at me through the wall on a winter night in the northeastern United States is most probably reverberating at the same moment in a dance hall in Bogotá, off a transistor in Narvik, via a jukebox in Kiev and an electric guitar in Bengazi. The tune is last month's or last week's top of the pops; already it has the whole of mass society for its echo chamber. The economics of this musical esperanto are staggering. Rock and pop breed concentric worlds of fashion, setting, and life style. Popular music has brought with it sociologies of private and public manner, of group solidarity. The politics of Eden come loud.

Many contexts of the decibel culture have been studied. What is more important, but difficult to investigate, let alone quantify, is the question of the development of mental faculties, of self-awareness, when these take place in a perpetual sound-matrix. What are the sweet, vociferous hammers doing to the brain at key stages in its development? We have no real precedent to tell us how life-forms mature and are conducted at anywhere near the levels of organized noise which now cascade through the day and the lit night (rock, in particular, bends and colors the light around it). When a young man walks down a street in Vladivostock or Cincinnati with his transistor blaring, when a car passes with its radio on at full blast, the resulting sound-capsule encloses the individual. It diminishes the external world to a set of acoustic surfaces. A pop regime imposes severe physical stress on the human ear. Some of the coarsening or damage that can follow has, in fact, been measured. But hardly anything is known of the psychological effects of saturation by volume and repetitive beat (often the same two or three tunes are played around the clock). What tissues of sensibility are being numbed or exacerbated?

Yet we are unquestionably dealing with a literacy, with codes of recognition so widespread and dynamic that they constitute a "metaculture." Popular music(s) have their semantics, their theory of genres, their intricate play-offs of esoteric against canonic types. Folk and pop, "trad music" and rock, count their several histories and corpus of legend. They show their relics. They number their old masters and rebels, their betrayers and high priests. Precisely as in classical literacy, so there are in the world of jazz or of rock 'n' roll degrees of initiation ranging from the vague empathies of the tyro (Latin on sundials) to the acid erudition of the scholiast. At the same time there is an age factor which makes the culture of pop more like modern mathematics and physics than the humanities. In their execution of and response to popular music the young have a tension-span, a suppleness of appropriation denied to the old. Part of the reason may be a straightforward organic degeneracy: the delicate receptors of the inner ear harden and grow opaque during one's twenties.

In short, the vocabularies, the contextual behavior-patterns of pop and rock, constitute a genuine lingua franca, a "universal dialect" of youth. Everywhere a sound-culture seems to be driving back the old authority of verbal order.

Classical music has a large part in this new presence of sound. Increasingly, I believe, it is penetrating the lives, the habits of attention and repose, of men and women who were once "bookish." In numerous homes the hi-fi components and the rack for long-playing records occupy the place of the library. High-fidelity reproduction and the LP are more than a mechanical gain. They have opened up, brought into easy range, a large territory of music, of tonality and lost form, accessible before only to the eye of the archivist. In many respects the quality of the modern phonograph makes of the private sitting room an idealized concert hall. It allows a new fastidiousness of listening: no alien coughs disturb, no shuffling of wet feet, no false notes. The long-playing record has changed the relations of the ear to musical time. Because they can be put on at one go, or with a minimum of interval, works in a large format—a Mahler symphony—or meshed sequences such as the *Goldberg Variations* can now be listened to integrally, at home, and also repeated or segmented at will. This flexible inter-

play between time notation in the musical piece and the
time flow in the listener's personal life can be at once arbitrary and illuminating. As is the entirely novel fact that
all music can now be heard at any hour and as domestic
background. Tape, radio, the phonograph, the cassette will
emit an unending stream of music, at any moment or circumstance of the day. This probably accounts for the industry in Vivaldi and the minor eighteenth century. It explains
the prodigality of the baroque and the preclassical chamber
ensemble in the LP catalogue. So much of this music was,
in fact, conceived as *Tafelmusik* and aural tapestry around
the busy room. But we now tend to employ the great modes
also as if they were background. If we so choose, we can
put on Opus 131 while eating the breakfast cereal. We can
play the *St. Matthew Passion* any hour or day of the week.
Again, the effects are ambiguous: there can be an unprecedented intimacy, but also a devaluation (*désacralization*).
A Muzak of the sublime envelops us.

Habits of the bibliophile—of the library-cormorant, as
Coleridge called him—have shifted to the collector of records and performances. The furtive manias, the condescen-
sions of expertness, the hunter's zeal which bore once on
first editions, colophons, the *in-octavo* of a remaindered
text, are common now among music lovers. There is a science and market in old pressings, in out-of-stock albums,
in worn 78s, as there has long been in used books. Cata-
logues of recordings and rare tapes are becoming as exegetic
as bibliographies. Particularly in America, the record and

music store will be where the bookstore was, or books will hang on, in uneasy coexistence, as part of a music emporium. Where the Victorians published pocket books for lovers, garlands of prose and rhyme for lovers to read aloud to one another or in whispered exchange, we issue records to seduce by, to spin when the fire is low in the grate. If Dante wrote the line now, crystallizing total passion and the world shut out, it would, I think, read: "and they listened no more that day."

The facts behind this "musicalization" of our culture, behind the shift of literacy and historical awareness from eye to ear (only some, even among serious listeners, can read the score), are fairly obvious. But the underlying motives are so complex, one is so much a part of the change, that I hesitate to put forward any explanation.

The new ideals of shared inner life, of participatory emotion and leisure, certainly play a part. Except in the practice of reading aloud, paterfamilias to household, or of the tome passed from hand to hand and read aloud from in turn, the act of reading is profoundly solitary. It cuts the reader off from the rest of the room. It seals the sum of his consciousness behind unmoving lips. Loved books are the necessary and sufficient society of the alone. They close the door on other presences and make of them intruders. There is, in short, a fierce privacy to print and claim on silence. These, precisely, are the traits of sensibility now most suspect. The bias of current sentiment points insistently towards gregariousness, towards a liberal sharing of emotions.

The "great good place" of approved dreams is one of to-getherness. The harsh hoarding of feelings, inside the reader's silence, is out. Recorded music matches the new ideals perfectly. Sitting near one another, in intermittent concentration, we partake of the flow of sound both individually and collectively. This is the liberating paradox. Unlike the book, the piece of music is immediate common ground. Our responses to it can be simultaneously private and social. Our delight banishes no one. We draw close while being, more compactly, ourselves. The mutual tide of empathies can be disheveled and frankly lazy. The sheer luster, the fortes or pianos of stereophonic reproduction in a private room can be narcotic. A good deal of classical music is, today, the opium of the good citizen. Nevertheless, the search for human contact, for states of being that are intense but do not shut out others, is real. It is a part of the collapse of classic egoism. Often music "speaks" to that search as printed speech does not.

Perhaps one may conjecture further. The lapse from ceremony and ritual in much of public and private behavior has left a vacuum. At the same time, there is a thirst for magical and "transrational" forms. The capacity of organized religion to satisfy this thirst diminishes. Matthew Arnold foretold that the "facts" of religion would be replaced by its poetry. Today, one feels that in many educated, but imperfectly coherent lives, that "poetry of religious emotion" is being provided by music. The point is not easy to demonstrate; it pertains to the interior climate of feeling.

But one does know of a good many individual and familial existences in which the performance or enjoyment of music has functions as subtly indispensable, as exalting and consoling, as religious practices might have, or might have had formerly. It is this indispensability which strikes one, the feeling (which I share) that there is music one cannot do without for long, that certain pieces of music rather than, say, books, are the talisman of order and of trust inside oneself. In the absence or recession of religious belief, close-linked as it was to the classic primacy of language, music seems to gather, to harvest us to ourselves.

Perhaps it can do so because of its special relation to the truth. Neither ontology nor aesthetics have satisfactorily enunciated that relation. But we feel it readily. At every knot, from the voices of pubic men to the vocabulary of dreams, language is close-woven with lies. Falsehood is inseparable from its generative life. Music can boast, it can sentimentalize, it can release springs of cruelty. But it does not lie. (Is there a lie, anywhere, in Mozart?) It is here that the affinities of music with needs of feeling which were once religious may run deepest.

Conceivably, an ancient circle is closing. In his *Mythologiques* Lévi-Strauss has asserted that melody holds the key to the "mystère suprème de l'homme." Grasp the riddle of melodic invention, of our apparently imprinted sense of harmonic accord, and you will touch on the roots of human consciousness. Only music, says Lévi-Strauss, is a primal universal language, at once comprehensible to all and untranslatable into any other idiom. Speech comes later than music; even before the disorder at Babel, it was part of the Fall of man. This supposition is, itself, immemorial. It is fundamental to Orphic and Pythagorean doctrines, to the *harmonia mundi* of Boethius and the sixteenth century. It guided Kepler and was inferred, almost as a commonplace, in Condillac's great *Essai sur l'origine des connaissances humaines* of 1746. It is no accident that the two visionaries most observant of the crises of the classic order, Kierkegaard and Nietzsche, should have seen in music the mode of preeminent energy and meaning. With the mendacities of language brought home to us by psychoanalysis and the mass media, it may be that music is regaining ancient ground, wrested from it, held for a time, by the dominance of the word.

In part these are metaphors and discursive myths. But the condition of feeling which they reflect is real. The literacies of popular and classical music, informed by new techniques of reproduction no less important than was the spread of cheap mass-printing in its time, are entering our lives at numerous, shaping levels. In many settings and sensibilities they are providing a "culture outside the word." This movement will, I expect, continue. We are too close to the facts to see them whole. The test of objectivity is, still, bound to be personal. In ways which are simple-minded but difficult to paraphrase, the "motion" of these lectures seeks to echo, to parallel by other means, a musical figure: a tentative upward arc and descent in the orchestra —it holds one's breath—towards the close of Bartók's *Bluebeard's Castle*. We seem to stand, in regard to a theory of culture, where Bartók's Judith stands when she asks to open the last door on the night.

For Matthew Arnold the touchstones of supreme civilization, of personal feeling in accord with the highest moral and intellectual values, were passages of Greek, Shakespearean, or Miltonic verse. One suspects that for many of us, now, the image of decisive recourse would be less a touchstone than a tuning fork. *Musique avant toute chose.*

If music is one of the principal "languages outside the word," mathematics is another. Any argument on a post-culture and on future literacy will have to address itself, decisively, to the role of the mathematical and natural sciences. Theirs may very soon be the central sphere. Statistics can be shallow or ambiguous in interpretation. But those which tabulate the growth of the sciences do, in plain fact, map a new world. More than 90 percent of all scientists known to human record are now living. The number of papers which may be regarded as relevant to an advance in chemistry, physics, and the biological sciences—that is, the recent, active literature in these three fields alone—is estimated as being in excess of three and a quarter million. The critical indices in the sciences—investment, publication, number of men trained, percentage of the gross national product directly implicated in research and devel-

these developments. Yet all but the last-mentioned are i
definite sight. That not one of these exploding horizor
should even appear in Eliot's analysis of culture indicate
the pace of mutation since 1948. Our ethics, our centra
habits of consciousness, the immediate and environmenta
membrane we inhabit, our relations to age and to remem
brance, to the children whose gender we may select an
whose heredity we may program, are being transformec
As in the twilit times of Ovid's fables of mutant being, w
are in metamorphosis. To be ignorant of these scientifi
and technological phenomena, to be indifferent to thei
effects on our mental and physical experience, *is to opt ou
of reason.* A view of post-classic civilization must, increas
ingly, imply a vision of the sciences, of the language-world
of mathematical and symbolic notation. Theirs is the com
manding energy: in material fact, in the "forward dreams'
which define us. Today, our dialectics are binary.

But the motives for trying to incorporate science int
the field of common reference, of imaginative reflex, ar
better than utilitarian. And this is so even if we take "utili
tarian," as we must, to include our very survival as a species
The true motives ought to be those of delight, of intellectua
energy, of moral venture. To have some personal rappor
with the sciences is, very probably, to be in contact with
that which has most force of life and comeliness in our
reduced condition.

At seminal levels of metaphor, of myth, of laughter,
where the arts and the worn scaffolding of philosophic

opment—are doubling every seven to ten years. Between
now and 1990, according to a recent projection, the number
of monographs published in mathematics, physics, chemistry, and biology will, if aligned on an imaginary shelf,
stretch to the moon. Less tangibly, but more significantly,
it has been estimated that some 75 percent of the most
talented individuals in the developed nations, of the men
and women whose measurable intelligence comes near the
top of the curve in the community, now work in the sciences.
Politics and the humanities thus seem to draw on a quarter
of the optimal mental resources in our societies, and recruit
largely from below the line of excellence. It is almost a
platitude to insist that no previous period in history offers
any parallel to the current exponential growth in the rate,
multiplicity, and effects of scientific-technological advance.
It is equally obvious that even the present fantastic pace
(interleaved, as it may be, by phases of disillusion or regrouping in certain highly developed nations) will at least
double by the early 1980s. This phenomenology brings with
it wholly unprecedented demands on information absorption and rational application. We stand less on that shore
of the unbounded which awed Newton, than amid tidal
movements for which there is not even a theoretic model.

One can identify half a dozen areas of maximal pressure,
points at which pure science and technological realization
will alter basic structures of both private and social life.

There is a galaxy of biomedical "engineering." Spare-
part surgery, the use of chemical agencies against the de-

generation of ageing tissues, preselection of the sex of the embryo, of the manipulation of genetic factors towards ethical or strategic ends—each of these literally prepare a new typology of man. So does the direct chemical or electrochemical control of behavior. By implanting electrodes in the brain, by giving personality-control drugs, the therapist will be able to program alterations of consciousness, he will touch on the electrochemistry of motive to determine the deed. Memory-transfer through biochemical transplant, for which controversial claims are now being made, would alter the essential relations of ego and time. Unquestionably, our current inroads on the human cortex dwarf all previous images of exploration.

The revolutions of awareness that will result from full-scale computerization and electronic data-processing can only be crudely guessed at. At some point in 1969 the information-handling capacity of computers—that is, the number of units of information which can be received and stored—passed that of the 3.5 billion brains belonging to the human race. By 1975, computers will be leading by a fifty to one ratio. By whatever criterion used—size of memory, cost, speed and accuracy of calculation—computers are now increasing a thousandfold every fifteen years. In advanced societies the electronic data-bank is fast becoming the pivot of military, economic, sociological, and archival procedures. Though a computer is a tool, its powers are such that they go far beyond any model of governed, easily limited instrumentality. Analogue and digital computeriza-

tion are transforming the relations of density, between the human intellect and available kn tween personal choice and projected possibilit to telephone lines or to more sophisticated arte mission, multipurpose computers will becon presence in all offices and most homes. It is p this electronic cortex will simultaneously redu larity of the individual and immensely enlarge tial and operational scope. Inevitably, the r issues of electronic storage and information- becoming the focus of the study of mind.

The fourth main area is that of large-sca modification. There is a good deal of millen and recoil from adult politics in the current pa environment. Nevertheless, the potentialities able. Control of weather, locally at least, is now As are the economic exploitation of the contin and of the deeper parts of the sea. Man's settin tive skin" is becoming malleable on a scale p imaginable. Beyond these fields lies space Momentary boredom with the smooth histri thing ought not to blur two crucial eventualit the establishment of habitable bases outside overcrowded or war-torn earth, and, remote as i the perception of signals from other systems of or information. Fontenelle's inspired speculati *Sur la pluralité des mondes* are now a statistical

We cannot hope to measure the sum and co

systems fail us, science is active. Touch on even its more abstruse regions and a deep elegance, a quickness and merriment of the spirit come through. Consider the Banach-Tarski theorem whereby the sun and a pea may be so divided into a finite number of disjoint parts that every single part of one is congruent to a unique part of the other. The undoubted result is that the sun may be fitted into one's vest pocket, and that the conponent parts of the pea will fill the entire universe solidly, no vacant space remaining either in the interior of the pea or in the universe. What surrealist fantasy yields a more precise wonder? Or take the Penrose theorem in cosmology, which tells us that under extreme conditions of gravitational collapse a critical stage is reached whereby no communication with the outside world is possible. Light cannot escape the pull of the gravitational field. A "black hole" develops, representing the locale of a body of near-zero volume and near-infinite density. Or, even more remarkably, the "collapse-event" may open "into" a new universe hitherto unapprehended. Here spin the *soleils noirs* of Baudelaire and romantic trance. But the marvelous wit is that of fact. Very recent observations of at least two bodies, a companion to the star Aur and the supergiant star Her 89, suggest that Penrose's model of a "hole in space" is true. "Constantly, I seek a poetry of facts," writes Hugh MacDiarmid:

> Even as
> The profound kinship of all living substance
> Is made clear by the chemical route.

Without some chemistry one is bound to remain
Forever a dumbfounded savage
In the face of vital reactions.
The beautiful relations
Shown only by biochemistry
Replace a stupefied sense of wonder
With something more wonderful
Because natural and understandable.

That "poetry of facts" and realization of the miraculous
delicacies of perception in contemporary science already
informs literature at those nerve-points where it is both
discplined and under the stress of the future. It is no accident that Musil was trained as an engineer, that Ernst
Jünger and Nabokov should be serious entymologists, that
Broch and Canetti are writers schooled in the exact and
mathematical sciences. The special, deepening presence of
Valéry in one's feelings about the afterlife of culture is inseparable from his own alertness to the alternative poetics,
to the "other metaphysics" of mathematical and scientific
pursuit. The instigations of Queneau and of Borges, which
are among the most bracing in modern letters, have algebra
and astronomy at their back. And there is a more spacious,
central instance. Proust's only successor is Joseph Needham.
A la recherche du temps perdu and *Science and Civilization
in China* represent two prodigiously sustained, controlled
flights of the re-creative intellect. They exhibit what Coleridge termed "esemplastic powers," that many-branched
coherence of design which builds a great house of language

for memory and conjecture to inhabit. The China of Needham's passionate recomposing—so inwardly shaped before he went in search of its material truth—is a place as intricate, as lit by dreams, as the way to Combray. Needham's account, in an "interim" essay, of the misreadings and final discovery of the true hexagonal symmetry of the snow-crystal has the same exact savor of manifold revealing as the Narrator's sightings of the steeple at Martinville. Both works are a long dance of the mind.

It is often objected that the layman cannot share in the life of the sciences. He is "bound to remain forever a dumbfounded savage" before a world whose primary idiom he cannot grasp. Though good scientists themselves rarely say this, it is obviously true. But only to a degree. Modern science is centrally mathematical; the development of rigorous mathematical formalization marks the evolution of a given discipline, such as biology, to full scientific maturity. Having no mathematics, or very little, the "common reader" is excluded. If he tries to penetrate the meaning of a scientific argument, he will probably get it muddled or misconstrue metaphor to signify the actual process. True again, but of a truth that is halfway to indolence. Even a modest mathematical culture will allow some approach to what is going on. The notion that one can exercise a rational literacy in the latter part of the twentieth century without a knowledge of calculus, without some preliminary access to topology or algebraic analysis, will soon seem a bizarre archaism. These styles and speech-forms from the grammar of number are already indispensable to many branches of modern logic, philosophy, linguistics, and psychology. They are the language of feeling where it is today, most adventurous. As electronic data-processing and coding pervade more and more of the economics and social order of our lives, the mathematical illiterate will find himself cut off. A new hierarchy of menial service and stunted opportunity may develop among those whose resources continue to be purely verbal. There may be "word-helots."

Of course, the mathematical literacy of the amateur must remain modest. Usually he will apprehend only a part of the scientific innovation, catching a momentary, uncertain glimpse of a continuum, making an approximate image for himself. But is this not, in fact, the way in which we view a good deal of modern art? Is it not precisely through intervals of selective appropriation, via pictorial analogies which are often naïve in the extreme, that the nonmusician assimilates the complex, ultimately technical realities of music?

The history of science, moreover, permits of a less demanding access, yet one that leads to the center. A modest mathematical culture is almost sufficient to enable one to follow the development of celestial mechanics and of the theory of motion until Newton and Laplace. (Has there been a subtler recapturer of motive, of the dart and recoil of mind, than Alexandre Koyré, the historian of this movement?) It takes no more than reasonable effort to understand at least along major lines, the scruple, the elegance

opment—are doubling every seven to ten years. Between now and 1990, according to a recent projection, the number of monographs published in mathematics, physics, chemistry, and biology will, if aligned on an imaginary shelf, stretch to the moon. Less tangibly, but more significantly, it has been estimated that some 75 percent of the most talented individuals in the developed nations, of the men and women whose measurable intelligence comes near the top of the curve in the community, now work in the sciences. Politics and the humanities thus seem to draw on a quarter of the optimal mental resources in our societies, and recruit largely from below the line of excellence. It is almost a platitude to insist that no previous period in history offers any parallel to the current exponential growth in the rate, multiplicity, and effects of scientific-technological advance. It is equally obvious that even the present fantastic pace (interleaved, as it may be, by phases of disillusion or regrouping in certain highly developed nations) will at least double by the early 1980s. This phenomenology brings with it wholly unprecedented demands on information absorption and rational application. We stand less on that shore of the unbounded which awed Newton, than amid tidal movements for which there is not even a theoretic model.

One can identify half a dozen areas of maximal pressure, points at which pure science and technological realization will alter basic structures of both private and social life.

There is a galaxy of biomedical "engineering." Spare-part surgery, the use of chemical agencies against the de-

these developments. Yet all but the last-mentioned are in definite sight. That not one of these exploding horizons should even appear in Eliot's analysis of culture indicates the pace of mutation since 1948. Our ethics, our central habits of consciousness, the immediate and environmental membrane we inhabit, our relations to age and to remembrance, to the children whose gender we may select and whose heredity we may program, are being transformed. As in the twilit times of Ovid's fables of mutant being, we are in metamorphosis. To be ignorant of these scientific and technological phenomena, to be indifferent to their effects on our mental and physical experience, *is to opt out of reason*. A view of post-classic civilization must, increasingly, imply a vision of the sciences, of the language-worlds of mathematical and symbolic notation. Theirs is the commanding energy: in material fact, in the "forward dreams" which define us. Today, our dialectics are binary.

But the motives for trying to incorporate science into the field of common reference, of imaginative reflex, are better than utilitarian. And this is so even if we take "utilitarian," as we must, to include our very survival as a species. The true motives ought to be those of delight, of intellectual energy, of moral venture. To have some personal rapport with the sciences is, very probably, to be in contact with that which has most force of life and comeliness in our reduced condition.

At seminal levels of metaphor, of myth, of laughter, where the arts and the worn scaffolding of philosophic systems fail us, science is active. Touch on even its more abstruse regions and a deep elegance, a quickness and merriment of the spirit come through. Consider the Banach-Tarski theorem whereby the sun and a pea may be so divided into a finite number of disjoint parts that every single part of one is congruent to a unique part of the other. The undoubted result is that the sun may be fitted into one's vest pocket, and that the conponent parts of the pea will fill the entire universe solidly, no vacant space remaining either in the interior of the pea or in the universe. What surrealist fantasy yields a more precise wonder? Or take the Penrose theorem in cosmology, which tells us that under extreme conditions of gravitational collapse a critical stage is reached whereby no communication with the outside world is possible. Light cannot escape the pull of the gravitational field. A "black hole" develops, representing the locale of a body of near-zero volume and near-infinite density. Or, even more remarkably, the "collapse-event" may open "into" a new universe hitherto unapprehended. Here spin the *soleils noirs* of Baudelaire and romantic trance. But the marvelous wit is that of fact. Very recent observations of at least two bodies, a companion to the star Aur and the supergiant star Her 89, suggest that Penrose's model of a "hole in space" is true. "Constantly, I seek a poetry of facts," writes Hugh MacDiarmid:

> Even as
> The profound kinship of all living substance
> Is made clear by the chemical route.

> Without some chemistry one is bound to remain
> Forever a dumbfounded savage
> In the face of vital reactions.
> The beautiful relations
> Shown only by biochemistry
> Replace a stupefied sense of wonder
> With something more wonderful
> Because natural and understandable.

That "poetry of facts" and realization of the miraculous delicacies of perception in contemporary science already informs literature at those nerve-points where it is both discplined and under the stress of the future. It is no accident that Musil was trained as an engineer, that Ernst Jünger and Nabokov should be serious entymologists, that Broch and Canetti are writers schooled in the exact and mathematical sciences. The special, deepening presence of Valéry in one's feelings about the afterlife of culture is inseparable from his own alertness to the alternative poetics, to the "other metaphysics" of mathematical and scientific pursuit. The instigations of Queneau and of Borges, which are among the most bracing in modern letters, have algebra and astronomy at their back. And there is a more spacious, central instance. Proust's only successor is Joseph Needham. *A la recherche du temps perdu* and *Science and Civilization in China* represent two prodigiously sustained, controlled flights of the re-creative intellect. They exhibit what Coleridge termed "esemplastic powers," that many-branched coherence of design which builds a great house of language for memory and conjecture to inhabit. The China of Needham's passionate recomposing—so inwardly shaped before he went in search of its material truth—is a place as intricate, as lit by dreams, as the way to Combray. Needham's account, in an "interim" essay, of the misreadings and final discovery of the true hexagonal symmetry of the snowcrystal has the same exact savor of manifold revealing as the Narrator's sightings of the steeple at Martinville. Both works are a long dance of the mind.

It is often objected that the layman cannot share in the life of the sciences. He is "bound to remain forever a dumbfounded savage" before a world whose primary idiom he cannot grasp. Though good scientists themselves rarely say this, it is obviously true. But only to a degree. Modern science is centrally mathematical; the development of rigorous mathematical formalization marks the evolution of a given discipline, such as biology, to full scientific maturity. Having no mathematics, or very little, the "common reader" is excluded. If he tries to penetrate the meaning of a scientific argument, he will probably get it muddled or misconstrue metaphor to signify the actual process. True again, but of a truth that is halfway to indolence. Even a modest mathematical culture will allow some approach to what is going on. The notion that one can exercise a rational literacy in the latter part of the twentieth century without a knowledge of calculus, without some preliminary access to topology or algebraic analysis, will soon seem a bizarre archaism. These styles and speech-forms from the grammar of number are already indispensable to many branches of modern logic, philosophy, linguistics, and psychology. They are the language of feeling where it is today, most adventurous. As electronic data-processing and coding pervade more and more of the economics and social order of our lives, the mathematical illiterate will find himself cut off. A new hierarchy of menial service and stunted opportunity may develop among those whose resources continue to be purely verbal. There may be "word-helots."

Of course, the mathematical literacy of the amateur must remain modest. Usually he will apprehend only a part of the scientific innovation, catching a momentary, uncertain glimpse of a continuum, making an approximate image for himself. But is this not, in fact, the way in which we view a good deal of modern art? Is it not precisely through intervals of selective appropriation, via pictorial analogies which are often naïve in the extreme, that the nonmusician assimilates the complex, ultimately technical realities of music?

The history of science, moreover, permits of a less demanding access, yet one that leads to the center. A modest mathematical culture is almost sufficient to enable one to follow the development of celestial mechanics and of the theory of motion until Newton and Laplace. (Has there been a subtler recapturer of motive, of the dart and recoil of mind, than Alexandre Koyré, the historian of this movement?) It takes no more than reasonable effort to understand at least along major lines, the scruple, the elegance of hypothesis and experiment which characterize the modulations of the concept of entropy from Carnot to Helmholz. The genesis of Darwinism and the subsequent reexaminations which lead from orthodox evolutionary doctrine to modern molecular biology are one of the "very rich hours" of the human intellect. Yet much of the material and of its philosophical implications are accessible to the layman. This is so, to a lesser degree, of some part of the debate between Einstein, Bohr, Wolfgang Pauli, and Max Born—from each of whom we have letters of matchless honesty and personal commitment—on the issue of anarchic indeterminacy or subjective interference in quantum physics. Here are topics as crowded with felt life as any in the humanities.

The absence of the history of science and technology from the school syllabus is a scandal. It is an absurdity to speak of the Renaissance without knowledge of its cosmology, of the mathematical dreams which underwrote its theories of art and music. To read seventeenth and eighteenth-century literature or philosophy without an accompanying awareness of the unfolding genius of physics, astronomy, and algebraic analysis during the period is to read only at the surface. A model of neo-Classicism which omits Linnaeus is hollow. What can be said responsibly of romantic historicism, of the new mappings of time after Hegel, which fails to include a study of Buffon, Cuvier, and Lamarck? It is not only that the humanities have been arrogant in their assertions of centrality. It is that they have often been silly. We need no poet more urgently than Lucretius.

Where culture itself is so utterly fragmented, there is no need to speak of the sciences as separate. What does make them so different from the present state of the humanities is their collectivity and inner calendar. Overwhelmingly, today, science is a collective enterprise in which the talent of the individual is a function of the group. But, as we have seen, more and more of current radical art and anti-art aspires to the same plurality. The really deep divergence between the humanistic and scientific sensibilities is one of temporality. Very nearly by definition, the scientist knows that tomorrow will be in advance of today. A twentieth-century schoolboy can manipulate mathematical and experimental concepts inaccessible to a Galileo or a Gauss. For a scientist the curve of time is positive. Inevitably, the humanist looks back. The essential repertoire of his consciousness, the props of his daily life as a scholar or critic are from the past. A natural bent of feeling will lead him to believe, perhaps silently, that the achievements of the past are more radiant than those of his own age. The proposition that "Shakespeare is the greatest, most complete writer mankind will ever produce" is a logical and almost a grammatical provocation. But it carries conviction. And even if a Rembrandt or a Mozart may, in future, be equaled (itself a gross, indistinct notion), they cannot be surpassed. There is a profound logic of sequent energy in the arts, but not an additive progress in the sense of the sciences. No errors are corrected or theorems disproved. Because it carries the past within it, language, unlike mathematics, draws backward. This is the meaning of Eurydice. Because the realness of his inward lies at his back, the man of words, the singer, will turn back, to the place of necessary beloved shadows. For the scientist time and the light lie before.

Here, if anywhere, lies division of the "two cultures" or, rather, of the two orientations. Anyone who has lived among scientists will know how intensely this polarity influences life style. Their evenings point self-evidently to tomorrow, *e santo è l'avvenir.*

Or is it really?

This is the last question I want to touch on. And by far the most difficult. I can state it and feel its extreme pressure. But I have not been able to think it through in any clear or consequent manner.

That science and technology have brought with them fierce problems of environmental damage, of economic unbalance, of moral distortion, is a commonplace. In terms of ecology and ideals of sensibility the cost of the scientific-technological revolutions of the past four centuries has been very high. But despite anarchic, pastoral critiques such as those put forward by Thoreau and Tolstoy, there has been little fundamental doubt that it ought to be met. In that largely unexamined assurance there has been a part of blind economic will, of the immense hunger for comfort and material diversity. But there has also been a much deeper mechanism: the conviction, centrally woven into the Western temper, at least since Athens, that mental inquiry must move forward, that such motion is natural and meritorious in itself, that man's proper relation to the truth is one of pursuer (the "haloo" of Socrates cornering his quarry rings through our history). We open the successive doors in Bluebeard's castle because "they are there," because each leads to the next by a logic of intensification which is that of the mind's own awareness of being. To leave one door closed would be not only cowardice but a betrayal—radical, self-mutilating—of the inquisitive, probing, forward-tensed stance of our species. We are hunters after reality, wherever it may lead. The risks, the disasters incurred are flagrant. But so is, or has been until very recently, the axiomatic assumption and a priori of our civilization, which holds that man and the truth are companions, that their roads lie forward and are dialectically cognate.

For the first time (and one's conjectures here will be tentative and blurred), this all-governing axiom of continued advance is being questioned. I am thinking of issues that go far beyond current worries in the scientific community about the environment, about weaponry, about the mindless applications of chemistry to the human organism. The real question is whether certain major lines of inquiry ought to be pursued at all, whether society and the human intellect at their present level of evolution can survive the next truths. It may be—and the mere possibility presents dilemmas beyond any which have arisen in history—that the coming door opens onto realities ontologically opposed to our sanity and limited moral reserves. Jacques Monod has asked publicly what many have puzzled over in private: Ought genetic research to continue if it will lead to truths about differentiations in the species whose moral, political, psychological consequences we are unable to cope with? Are we free to pursue neurochemical or psychophysiological spoors concerning the layered, partially archaic forms of the cortex, if such study brings the knowledge that ethnic hatreds, the need for war, or those impulses toward self-ruin hinted at by Freud are inherited facts? Such examples can be multiplied.

It may be that the truths which lie ahead wait in ambush for man, that the kinship between speculative thought and survival on which our entire culture has been based, will break off. The stress falls on "our" entire culture because, as anthropologists remind us, numerous primitive societies have chosen stasis or mythological circularity over forward motion, and have endured around truths immemorially posited.

The notion that abstract truth, and the morally neutral truths of the sciences in particular, might come to paralyze or destroy Western man is foreshadowed in Husserl's *Krisis der europäischen Wissenschaften* (1934-37). It becomes a dominant motif in the theory of "negative dialectic" of Horkheimer, Adorno, and the Frankfurt School. This is one of the most challenging, though often hermetic, currents in modern feeling and in the modern diagnosis of the crisis of culture. Tito Perlini's long essay, *Autocritica della ragione illuministica* (in *Ideologie* 9/10 [1969]) is not only a lucid introduction to this material but a stringent statement of the case.

Reason itself has become repressive. The worship of "truth" and of autonomous "facts" is a cruel fetishism: "Elevato ad idolo di se stesso, il *fatto* è un tiranno assoluto di fronte a cui il pensiero non può non posternasi in. muta adorazione."* The disease of enlightened man is his acceptance, itself wholly superstitious, of the superiority of facts to ideas. "La spinta al *positivo* è tentazione mortale per la cultura."† Instead of serving human ends and spontaneities, the "positive truths" of science and of scientific laws have become a prison house, darker than Piranesi's, a *carcere* to imprison the future. It is these "facts," not man, which regulate the course of history. As Horkheimer and Adorno emphasize in the *Dialektik der Aufklärung*, the old obscurantisms of religious dogma and social caste have been replaced by the even more tyrannical obscurantism of "rational, scientific truth." "Reality has the better of ideology," writes Perlini, meaning that a myth of objective, verifiable scientific evidence has overwhelmed the utopian, fundamentally anarchic springs of humane consciousness: "In nome di un'esperienza ridotta al simulacro

---

**Raised to the status of an autonomous idol, the* fact *is an absolute tyrant before whom thought can do nothing but bow down in silent worship.*
†*The thrust towards* the positive *is a fatal temptation for culture.*

di se stessa, viene condanatta come vuota fantasticheria la
stessa capacità soggettiva di progettazione dell'uomo."*
   The vigor of the indictment, its moral and intellectual
attractions, are evident. But so are its weaknesses. It is no
accident that Horkheimer and Adorno were unable to complete the *Dialektik*. Nowhere do we find substantive examples of how a liberated, "multidimensional" man would
in fact restructure his relations to reality, to that "which is
so." Where is the actual program for a mode of human
perception freed from the "fetishism of abstract truth"?
   But the argument is flawed at a more elemental level.
The pursuit of the facts, of which the sciences merely provide the most visible, organized instance, is no contingent
error embarked on by Western man at some moment of
élitist or bourgeois rapacity. That pursuit is, I believe, imprinted on the fabric, on the electrochemistry and impulse-
net of our cortex. Given an adequate climatic and nutritive
milieu, it was bound to evolve and to augment by a constant
feedback of new energy. The partial absence of this quest-
ing compulsion from less-developed, dormant races and
civilizations does not represent a free choice or feat of innocence. It represents, as Montesquieu knew, the force of
adverse ecological and genetic circumstance. The flower
child in the Western city, the neoprimitive chanting his
five words of Thibetan on the highway are performing an

---

*In the name of experience, itself diminished to a mere figment, man's
very capacity for personal, subjective innovation is condemned as being
no more than an empty fantasy.*

infantile charade, founded on the surplus wealth of that same city or highway. We cannot turn back. We cannot choose the dreams of unknowing. We shall, I expect, open the last door in the castle even if it leads, perhaps *because* it leads, onto realities which are beyond the reach of human comprehension and control. We shall do so with that desolate clairvoyance, so marvelously rendered in Bartók's music, because opening doors is the tragic merit of our identity.

There are two obvious responses to this outlook. There is Freud's stoic acquiescence, his grimly tired supposition that human life was a cancerous anomaly, a detour between vast stages of organic repose. And there is the Nietzschean gaiety in the face of the inhuman, the tensed, ironic perception that we are, that we always have been, precarious guests in an indifferent, frequently murderous, but always fascinating world:

> Schild der Notwendigkeit.
> Höchstes Gestirn des Seins!
> —das kein Wunsch erreicht,
> —das kein Nein befleckt,
> ewiges Ja des Seins,
> ewig bin ich dein Ja:
> den ich liebe dich, o Ewigkeit!*

Both attitudes have their logic and direction of conduct. One chooses or alternates between them for uncertain rea-

*Shield of Necessity. / Highest constellation of Being! / Which no desire can attain, / Which no negation can taint, / Eternal Yes of Being, / I am your lasting Affirmation: / For I love you, oh Eternity!

sons of private feeling, of authentic or imagined individual circumstance. Personally, I feel most drawn to the *gaia scienza*, to the conviction, irrational, even tactless as it may be, that it is enormously interesting to be alive at this cruel, late stage in Western affairs. If a *dur désir de durer* was the mainspring of classic culture, it may well be that our post-culture will be marked by a readiness not to endure rather than curtail the risks of thought. To be able to envisage possibilities of self-destruction, yet press home the debate with the unknown, is no mean thing.

But these are only indistinct guesses. It is no rhetorical move to insist that we stand at a point where models of previous culture and event are of little help. Even the term *Notes* is too ambitious for an essay on culture written at this moment. At most, one can try to get certain perplexities into focus. Hope may lie in that small exercise. "A blown husk that is finished," says Ezra Pound of man and of himself as he, the master-voyager of our age, nears a homecoming:

> A blown husk that is finished
>   but the light sings eternal
> a pale flare over marshes
>   where the salt hay whispers to tide's change.

(September 1970/January 1971)